LOOK
HERE

LOOK HERE

On the Pleasures of Observing the City

ANA KINSELLA

This edition first published in the United Kingdom
in 2022 by Daunt Books Originals
83 Marylebone High Street
London W1U 4QW

2

A CIP catalogue record for this title is
available from the British Library.

ISBN 978-1-914198-12-0

Typeset by Marsha Swan
Printed and bound by TJ Books Ltd

www.dauntbookspublishing.co.uk

Rarely have I felt more charmed
than on Ninth Street, watching a woman
stop in the middle of the sidewalk
to pull up her hair like it's
an emergency – and it is.

Alex Dimitrov, 'June'

This place multiplies when you're not looking.

Colson Whitehead,
The Colossus of New York

CONTENTS

PROLOGUE
From King's Cross to Holborn

In a single hour walking through central London I see the following: A teenage boy who bops with curiosity the dough-nut bun in the hair of the girl walking with him. A bride in a strapless white meringue of a dress who leaves Camden Town Hall, the two women close behind her working with military efficiency to keep her train out of puddles. A young woman who holds hands with a man whose other hand is holding a trumpet. It dangles from his wrist in a way that strikes me as almost dangerous in its carelessness. A trio of young girls in accessorised versions of school uniform – a neon scrunchie around an ankle sock, a small embellished bag for a mobile phone around the neck. A man in a light-grey suit who comes rushing out of a hotel near the British Museum, hand raised for a taxi, but the only one nearby speeds off. As I pass, his hand falls to his side with a familiar resignation.

None of these sights is remarkable. These are all just people doing what I'm doing: making their way through the city. But when I start to observe them, I notice more and more about them, and about the city, too. These are just strangers, yes, but when I pass them on the street, a window opens and for a fleeting moment I can see a small part of their lives. It might not seem like a part big enough to be interesting. It likely is only interesting enough to last a moment − the length of time it takes for me to pass them. As I walk, I lose my way, meandering rather than taking the direct route. I'm looking for people to look at, I think. Over and over, as I cross paths with these strangers, something of the city opens up to me, too.

Here we all are, the message seems to be, all of us part of an endless stream of personhood, of possibility.

1. Walking

There is very little logic to how London is laid out. You could be forgiven for getting lost. There is no grid, no structure to explain the way the streets run. Even the river coils its way through the city like an old-fashioned telephone cord. When I was very small, my family briefly lived on a quiet street perpendicular to the Thames. Kenyon Street was one of a ladder of quiet streets between the river and Fulham Palace Road, and later on my mother told me that they were known as the Alphabet Streets, their names running in alphabetical order, south to north. When I moved back to the city at twenty-two, I looked this up in my copy of the London A–Z to see if it was true. From Bishop's Park north to Hammersmith: Cloncurry, Doneraile, Ellerby, Finlay, Greswell, Harbord, Inglethorpe, Kenyon, Langthorne, Queensmill, Lysia, Niton. Wait, hang on a second. Where exactly did that Q come from?

Often, when navigating London, there is a sensation of the rug being pulled from under you.

Phyllis Pearsall, the painter and writer credited with creating much of London's modern street atlas – the *A to Z*, was familiar with the confusion of the city's streets. From a pedestrian's point of view, London can be difficult to make sense of. The A–Z's backstory states that after getting lost on her way to a party in Belgravia in the 1930s, Pearsall, a divorcee in her late twenties and the daughter of a map-maker, took the most up-to-date London map she could find and set out to improve it.

She did this by rising every day at 5 a.m. in her bedsit near Victoria station to walk for eighteen hours, noting places of interest, house numbers, side streets and main roads. Over time, she walked 3,000 miles over 23,000 streets. The map she developed divided London into smaller, more detailed sections, making its streets easier to navigate. Pearsall established the Geographers' A–Z Map Company to publish her street atlas, the *A to Z: Atlas and Guide to London and Suburbs with House Numbers*, with its distinctive red and blue cover, and she gave the company a motto in the form of a personal maxim of hers: On we go.

Pearsall's earliest iteration of the book hit a stumbling block soon after publication: once the Second World War began, maps of such a detailed scale could no longer be sold, due to the risk of local intelligence falling into enemy hands. Pearsall passed the war working in the Ministry of Information, making maps of the frontlines of battle, eventually fracturing her spine in an air accident while bringing a shipment of maps from the Netherlands.

Since her death in 1996 there has been debate over the veracity of the origin story of Pearsall's A–Z. For one thing, the map that resulted from all her walking claimed to include 9,000 more streets than any other. That was certainly a falsehood. It's a romantic idea, the image of Pearsall the footloose divorcee on her way to a party, the bohemian painter pounding pavements in a pair of sensible shoes, giving form to the chaos of London's twisted streets and neighbourhoods – as is Pearsall's fabled line of delivering early copies to W. H. Smith in a borrowed wheelbarrow. The romance of it all occludes the fact that it's probable that Pearsall was a master marketer more than she was a pioneering cartographer. But the success of her work does point to an indisputable truth, that London is a labyrinth, one in need of decoding if we are to make sense of it for ourselves.

Today all of this is a little easier. Almost everyone has a map more detailed and powerful than Pearsall's A–Z in their pockets, all the time. It's difficult, though not impossible, to get properly lost when you have Google Maps at your fingertips. But when I came to London as a student I didn't have a smartphone, and I moved through the city at the mercy of the countdown timer at the bus stop and my own errant sense of direction. I pinned a Tube map to the noticeboard above my desk and crossed through a station's name the first time I entered or exited it. From the very beginning, I found myself entranced by the breadth and depth of the city. Here was a thing so layered and complex that it had grown gnarled, and it was up to me to put myself inside of it. I knew that to move through it would be to move through time itself. I am the index, I thought, crossing out names on my Tube map. On we go.

As my knowledge of the city grew – which neighbourhoods had trees full of parakeets, where the good and peaceful pubs were – memory constructed something organic in my mind that I could call upon at a moment's notice: a map of my very own.

My first year in London was spent in anonymous student accommodation in the East End. It was my first time away from my family, my friends, and the freedom gave me the feeling of leaning over a balcony rail at a great height. I was fine. I was safe. But the precipice always loomed beneath me. The precipice was loneliness, and although I made new friends, I spent most evenings alone, cooking dinner and eating it while reading or studying in my bedroom. I wasn't lonely, but the fear of loneliness never quite left.

But walking was a kind of loneliness by choice. It was something more like solitude. Going by foot instead of public transport turned the journey into an undertaking, or maybe a lesson. And anyway, you were not alone on the street.

Even when I was lost in thought – about homesickness, or career prospects, or whether my new friends liked me or vice versa, or whether I was a good person or not – I was tuned to the frequency of the street by necessity. My personal morality, the rules and codes that governed how I thought I should live, gave way to the morality of the street. The street has its own codes, determined by those who walk it, and to go out among these strangers is to agree to take part in whatever the street might have in store. My own memories, history, fears, were replaced by those of the city's populace. What I received on that strange new wavelength was always astounding, or amusing, or just something. I queued for an ATM at South Kensington station behind a gentleman dressed as an astronaut. I watched him make two withdrawals amounting to £800. Taking a wrong turn down an Islington side street, I crossed paths with a group of off-duty street musicians who exploded in spontaneous music together, their day's work over. Two women danced arm in arm while the others passed around a bottle. Every instance like this became marked on the map in my mind, so much so that if one of my new friends had brought up South Kensington or Islington High Street, I would have had to bite my tongue to keep from blurting out what I'd seen there.

I found it impossible to be truly lonely when walking. It was impossible to dwell on my problems when I was pacing down Pentonville Road, making my way eastbound from King's Cross after class. Walking in London was a form of connection. I was new here, and I needed to learn what exactly the city was like. I did that by making a network, connecting the dots on foot. Like a path tramped by walkers through a field, my image of London emerged from my journeys across it. A trip to a new area opened something up in my mind: possibility, maybe, or even sometimes just the distraction of novelty. Away from the map my life was insecure and unstable – I was earning little, unsure about the future, frightened by the possibility of it all collapsing and my being forced to return to Ireland in the grip of a recession. I didn't know what the next day might bring, and the unknown was daunting. Better, then, to approach the unknown on my own terms – take a new route home from work, choose side streets instead of main roads and see what I might find.

As I did this, the only constant was that the city always found new things to show me.

These were little, incidental things. Things of almost no significance, things that popped up and made a tiny mark on my knowledge of London. They were anecdotes that lost their power the moment I tried to retell them. They were usually people – the sight of a well-dressed woman in her sixties reading *The Art Newspaper* on the train, lying to her colleague on the phone that she was about to go through a tunnel and then giving me a sly wink. They often had a pleasing synchronicity to them – two teenage boys who idly kicked a football in the park, hands backwards on their hips while they chatted. Over the course of an hour they drifted in a semicircle as the ball moved back and forth between them. On their own these incidents were barely noticeable, but when hung together like a string of pearls they started to carry a particular weight and rhythm of their own.

Whatever else happened during that first strange year in London, the time spent walking the city's streets alone did something to me. It changed me. Some people move to a new city and get a dramatic haircut, alter their personality, choose different kinds of lovers. I just went out walking. I wanted to learn what the city was like. In the process, something within me splintered open, and the way I looked at the world itself changed for good.

A chance encounter or observation is not just a single event. It doesn't occur in isolation. What I learned on my early walks is that the city does not stop. The Thames keeps rolling, whether anyone is there to watch it or not. At all hours of the day, couples would fight or reconcile on the bench outside my bedroom window. Shopkeepers would exercise small acts of kindness for their customers, or maybe they would not. Commuters would bump into each other on the train platform, distracted by their respective phones, and then catch themselves looking up from their screens to smile. On one occasion, I am walking in Mayfair, and just off Piccadilly I see two carpet merchants unfurl a huge Persian rug, larger than the square footage of my bedroom, right there on the dusty street. They stand back to appraise it, two men who know how to see the monetary value in a piece of art. Soon it becomes obvious to me: to move through London concentrating only on myself and my own movements would not just be short-sighted, it would be negligent.

The New York urbanist and writer Jane Jacobs gave this activity a name. She labelled it the 'intricate sidewalk ballet' that is particular to good city life. In her neighbourhood of Greenwich Village in the 1950s, it starts early in the morning with the clanging of rubbish bins and the passage of students on their way to class. Over the course of the day it gives way to longshoremen who drink and chat on street corners, executives lunching in bistros and the arrival of 'character dancers' – the old man carrying strings of shoes on his shoulders, or the bikers and their girlfriends who zip down the street. The ballet, Jacobs writes, reaches its peak after work when the street is filled with children at play and teenagers preening on stoops. In the evening the spotlights come on and the bars grow noisy, the delis visited by night workers looking for sandwiches.

The only way to know this sidewalk ballet, Jacobs says, is to play a role in it. It can't be known from afar, and those who merely watch from the wings will always get it a little wrong, 'like the old prints of rhinoceroses made from travelers' descriptions of rhinoceroses'. Before I moved to London I had a particular idea of what the city would be like to live in – what I might do, see or experience once there. I had the feeling, common to people in their early twenties about to make a big life change, that everything was waiting for me and that all I had to do was get there. Inevitably, I was wrong. After college I moved to London to write about clothes. I came to do a masters at a prestigious art school and, I hoped, to work for some of the fashion magazines I had read for so many years in my teenage bedroom. Those magazines had painted a picture of life in London as glamorous and exciting, teeming with novelty and celebrity and opportunity – all the things my life thus far had lacked.

The reality was at once less glamorous and more entrancing. On those walks around London, I learned what the city was made of: pavements and streets, networks both physical and emotional. Layers of lives on top of each other – a pub that used to be a corner shop, which used to be accommodation for local workers, overlooking a quiet street where children played and dogs were walked and where adults argued, did favours for each other, remained in love with each other or ceased to be so. Cities, conventional wisdom states, are places for money and opportunity. But what I learned when I started working and writing for those magazines, the ones I used to read in my bedroom, was that there was no room for real observation; not in the form I wanted, anyway. Working according to the dictates of the fashion industry was stultifying in its narrowness. Magazines depend on brands for their revenue, and brands only push their product for a certain kind of consumer. As time went by, I realised that I didn't see people as consumers. I saw them as people. I still loved looking at them – noticing what they were wearing, what little decisions they had made about how they presented themselves to the world and what that said about who they were. Yet all of that, I learned, had very little to do with fashion itself. If I wanted to look – to really observe the people in the city all around me – it would have to be on my own terms and nobody else's.

Time passed, and without noticing, I had spent the best part of my twenties working in an industry with which I felt constantly at odds. It came to a point where I realised I wanted to turn away from it. But I wasn't ready to abandon my love of looking. Instead I tried to carve out space for joy, to seek and find those glimmering moments of chance and coincidence unique to city life. They came to me as observations of the most minor moments: a stranger's citrus-coloured socks on the Tube, or the way a woman might stop on a street corner to fix her ponytail. These small, insignificant things felt nourishing to me – beautiful, even – in a way nothing in my job did. That realisation gnawed at me. I had derived so much of my place in London from my job. It was, in a sense, my purpose here. What would I do without it?

As time went on, I dawdled more. Looked harder. One July evening, I took the scenic route home from my office in Hackney, crossing Hampstead Heath in the last of the day's sunshine. At the summit of Parliament Hill, I paused and looked out at the city skyline. I thought to myself: it's like a painting, and then realised that if it was, it was because this is where people come to make those paintings. I'd seen them here myself many times before on sunny days. People who pack up their watercolours and their portable easels, climb the side of the hill, take a seat, and spend hours recreating what they see before them. That's how it works. I decided then to quit my job and pursue other work, and spend more time walking the city and writing about it, too, if I could afford it, seeking out new perspectives, other stories. A step into the unknown, perhaps, but after so many steps along so many unknown streets, I felt ready. On we go, I said under my breath. I walked back down the hill alone, watching my feet underneath me, pounding a path for myself with each step.

2. In Chinatown

After the screening at the Barbican's film festival, my partner Karl and I walk into town and go to our usual spot in Chinatown for dinner, a crowded upstairs room where the food is cheap and delicious, and the service reliably rude. The round tables here are shared, though ours is empty when we take our seats. Soon a couple is sat down beside us. They're in their seventies and have that look that couples get when they have been together for decades – they're not dressed alike but are certainly in sync with each other. Lightweight dark turtlenecks and city trousers, quilted coats that seem smart, rather than country. They don't acknowledge us. The man orders two bottles of beer.

'This beer,' he says to the waitress. 'We've been coming here for years and years, and we always have this beer.'

She doesn't care. She just nods and walks towards the kitchen.

They fuss for several minutes with their bags, ensuring they're safe from being pickpocketed (they are), and then she helps him choose a dish that's in line with his various dietary requirements, and finally they settle.

The two of us eat in silence, and so I watch all of this from across the table. It is comforting to watch their tender practicality, their long-term togetherness. What is it about love and friendship that spans the decades like this? On a dark cold evening in the crowded city, it appears like a neon sign in a window to say something like this: there are always ways to be happy together. There are ways that can last a very long time.

When I was younger the idea of being with someone so long that you started to dress like them seemed a bit silly. It made me want to ask, who are you really? Has some part of you got lost along the way? Now, enduring togetherness is a balm in what can be a lonely city. I look for it when I move through London. It's the higher standard to which I wish to hold myself: the two friends in their sixties who gossip about *The Archers* in the Ethiopian restaurant on a cold evening, legs crossed under the table, hand-knit scarves and hats piled high on the bench beside them. The pair of middle-aged men in the front row at the Tate's screening of Christian Marclay's *The Clock* on a weekday morning, who stay from opening until noon and then leave immediately, one pulling a Twix from an anorak pocket to share on the way out.

Once you start to look for it, you can see it everywhere. What a relief. At some point each pair seems to make a decision – whether all at once or over years – to stick close regardless of the difficulties life throws up. Enduring togetherness, whether romantic or otherwise. There is such power in it. A kind of radical alternative to the impossibility presented by London, the loneliness that can be fomented here.

* * *

I have been living in London for almost a decade. Spend long enough in one place and the desire to identify waymarkers becomes greater. Time passing can blur into haze. The past becomes impressionistic, painted in strokes that gesture at the truth rather than represent it accurately, like the image of a city street in the dark, seen through a rainy window.

So I find myself looking for the waymarkers, the individual brushstrokes that gradually become load-bearing as they make up a portrait.

One: I am walking through Cavendish Square in the early dusk of a midwinter afternoon. It is an unremarkable space, just north of Oxford Circus, a wide patch of grass covering a subterranean multistorey car park. A slant of low sunlight falls from beyond the imposing bulk of the John Lewis building and as I turn a corner on the path, it blinds me for a moment. Then I am reminded of another time I walked through this square, on my way home from a meeting, on the phone to a friend with whom I no longer speak. I remember who I was on that day, what I wore. I was the same woman I am now, but smaller, more afraid. Without the knowledge that I have now. A quieter voice, less sure of myself. I remember that it was late spring and warm, so the sunlight that momentarily blinds me today was higher in the sky. I had on a navy-blue pleated skirt and cream leather jazz shoes. I remember my friend telling me that she had been fired, or else maybe broken up with, and asking me to meet her in the pub. I paused for only a second before turning around and marching back towards the Tube that would take me to her.

Two: I am on a bus that drives past a flat where I used to live, and the windows of the flat are all open. There is a young woman leaning with her forearms on the balcony, just where I used to lean on mine. She is alone, but the sight of her makes me remember sitting on that balcony with a former flat-mate, eating ice creams on the chairs we'd dragged outside from the kitchen. A hot night, both of us with our legs bare, talking through each other's problems. The peculiar way that solving another person's problems has always made my own seem more manageable. The woman on the balcony is three storeys up and I wonder if she is working through a problem of her own. I would like to tell her that they always seem worse when you are by yourself.

Writing about his own return to New York, the city he grew up in, Henry James called these locations or buildings scattered around the city 'terrible traps to memory', which he thought could catch a person in a snare while walking down a street. The phrase makes me think of the hatch doors you find in that city's sidewalks, the ones that cover stairs leading down to cellars below. How the sight of something having changed on a street can make the observer feel suddenly the weight of her years, the passing of all that time. She tumbles down, alone, into the dark. Some raw combination of images, scenes, emotions that can reach back through the years of a person's life, unearthing an artefact of feeling buried long ago.

Memory is a mess on its own. It is difficult to grasp or make sense of. My memories instead become woven with place, with time of day, with an item of clothing or a person's voice on the other end of the line. In this way my life in London began to arrange itself into little stories, threads of narrative that pulsed around the city, stitching over each other again and again. It is impossible to extricate from the map it has woven for itself.

Three: It's a bright, brisk morning, early spring. I have a breakfast meeting in Soho, and afterwards I decide to walk to the office. The city has an air about it, like something has been released, or some forgotten tension has snapped. It's the funny time of day when most commuters are settled into their desks, and when the deliveries to Chinatown's restaurants are in full swing. Otherwise the streets are strangely empty. This is an area I know better after dark, in fractured memories of nights out from years ago, or from getting lost in the warren of streets around Old Compton Street on the way to a dinner. Looking for the right bus stop, ducking into the 24-hour supermarket to bring home a frozen pizza to my flatmates. The unexpected sight of a friend walking in the other direction across the street, on her way to another party. If I am never here again, if this is my last time walking down Shaftesbury Avenue, this would be enough, I think, the strange collusion of a spring morning and a million past evenings where it felt like something – something – was just about to begin.

NABIHAH IQBAL

Musician and broadcaster

What was London like when you were growing up? What did you do for fun?

A lot of live music. I started going to gigs when I was thirteen: the Astoria, the Mean Fiddler. I've got a lot of memories from then and now those places are all gone. I grew up close to Camden, so every weekend I'd be there, going to loads of punk and metal gigs. Me and all my friends were quite alternative.

Did you and your friends care about what was cool then?

Oh yeah. All of us were really into music. And I think music and fashion have always been synchronised, throughout different youth movements and things. So the way you looked – then, more than now – really mattered, because that was pre-smartphone and pre-Instagram and pre-internet, basically. The late nineties, early 2000s – the way that you looked then was basically your message out to the world. You know, it was very territorial in a way.

I'd be classed as what were called grungers. The opposite was a townie. I feel like everything is more fluid nowadays. And you don't see as many goths or punks in Camden nowadays. One of my best friends was a goth, but I was more of a punk. So we used to buy all our clothes in Camden Market. My best friend and I loved those big Criminal Damage trousers – do you know them? We made a pact that we would keep wearing these really big trousers for the rest of our lives, because they were so cool. The ones with the straps.

Do you still wear them now?

Oh, no. No! Definitely not. But I used to wear those with a hoodie of whichever band. A lot of jewellery, a spiky dog-collar necklace. I don't want to see any photos of that time now.

Is there anything from that time that affects how you dress now?

When I think about the way I dressed, for me it was always a way of standing out. At school having Dr. Martens instead of Kickers was a signifier. Now I just want to wear clothes that are comfy, but that still stand out a bit. Not because they stand out – but more because I like them.

Did you always know you wanted to work in music?

Well, I always loved music, but I never planned to do it as a career. I actually did law before music and, you know, if you've got Asian immigrant parents, there's so much emphasis on education, getting certain jobs. So my parents really thought I'd become a barrister, and then I ditched all of that to focus on music.

Did you work as a barrister first?
I got called to the bar. And then after that I was working with women's rights lawyers in Cape Town, but I didn't do the last part of the pupillage.

Did you always want to stay in London, where you grew up?
I've been lucky enough to travel, through my music, and spend time in different places. I feel like London is the best example of a multicultural city. When you look at other European capitals – nowhere else even comes close, in terms of creating this vibrant community of all different types of people living side by side and getting on, just creating this patchwork where anyone can feel like they belong.

Then there's also the fact that it's beautiful, and it's historical, and my whole life is kind of woven into this city. You think about the other people's lives that are also woven in here – that's something I always think about when I cross the river. You're on Waterloo Bridge, you have this vista in front of you, and then you look at the city. And it is this monolith. It's really still and really big – it looks like a picture. But you know that what you're looking at is millions of people and millions of stories, and all of it connects over time.

And you also spend a lot of time in Pakistan.

I love it there. I just feel healthier. Because I'm resting. And I'm in my natural habitat. You know, for a lot of second-generation immigrant people here – we often forget that this is really not the climate that we're genetically supposed to live in. I always wear Pakistani clothes when I'm there. And I love wearing them because they're so colourful and comfortable. When you look at the actual garments, the cut of the pieces is so different and unusual compared to Western clothing.

In London I wear a lot of camo and military clothes, berets and stuff. I've worn camo since I was a teenager, and sometimes I go a bit overboard with it. I end up looking like a little soldier. Sometimes you get a lot of looks from men, like they're thinking, 'Why are you dressed like that?' But it just makes me feel strong.

Do you have different berets?

I have got different berets.

In the photos I've seen of you, they're always big.

Well, this one I'm wearing today is oversized. I've got a bunch. I love wearing hats – I feel like people don't wear them as much now. You look at old photos of crowds, and everyone was wearing a hat. Hats transform your whole look really easily. Nicholas, my partner, is the same too. He always wears hats. The beret thing started because me and my best friend Louise – she was the goth – we both started wearing berets in sixth form. And we both still wear them now!

Nicholas is a fashion designer. How long have you guys known each other?

It's eight years this year.

Can you remember what you were wearing when you first met?

Yes, I can – I have this weird thing in my memory where I can remember what anyone is wearing on a specific day. I always pay so much attention to clothes, it's just a weird thing I do. I was putting on a club night and he came through to the club. I was wearing an outfit that I'd made myself. I've stopped making clothes for myself now that I'm going out with Nicholas – because he always turns them inside out and says, 'What the hell? What is this hem? You didn't even zigzag it!'

But that night I'd made this two-piece brocade outfit, a crop-top blouse with a high-waist miniskirt. Pink and gold, trippy, 1960s pattern. He was wearing black trousers with black braces and a white t-shirt. He looked really cool.

Has going out with him influenced how you dress, other than stopping your dreams of making your own clothes?

It's made me think about clothes and fashion in a completely new way. You see behind the scenes of making clothes, sourcing natural fabrics, getting them made properly. All the attention to detail that goes into it. So now I think about quality more. Buying better things that might cost more, but that are better made. But we've influenced each other, too. Last weekend I got ready and was wearing this leopard-print shirt from Nepenthes, a shop we both like just off the Euston

Road. And then he went and put on the same shirt because he has the same one. I was like, 'What are you doing? I put it on first!' When I first met him, there was no way he would have ever worn leopard print. So that's my influence.

His influence on me is about appreciating different cuts and silhouettes. One thing that I think is so important as a female and wearing clothes is to not fall into the trap of thinking that wearing fewer clothes, or tighter clothes, is going to make you look better. Because I feel like that's the default way a lot of girls think, it's what we're told. But when you go to a country like Pakistan, for example, or Japan, the women there are super stylish, they're in interesting clothes, but it's not about showing your body so much. It's about different proportions and silhouettes. That's something that Nicholas really believes in too. There's not one way to look attractive. Sometimes I'll come in wearing massive trousers and a big coat and he'll be like, 'Oh wow, you look so nice!'

3. At the lido

The changing room at the pre-war lido is housed in a long concrete hall, each side lined with a row of little wooden cubicles painted in alternating primary colours. Almost all are empty when I arrive for my swim after work on a summer evening. So I choose one at random – yellow – and commence the awkward dance of changing into my swimsuit. The cubicle is open, but this is a changing room, of course, which means I should be brave enough to show whatever part of my naked body I need to.

In the cubicle, I have a moment of commune with my body as I pull off my shorts and t-shirt: the body my body has become over the years, a site of mystery and change but crucially, mine. I am stepping into my royal-blue swimsuit, shimmying the straps up over my breasts and onto my shoulders – the soft, smooth nylon at odds with the haphazard and fallible shell of my own skin – and my reverie is interrupted. Two girls, pre-teens at the meanest point of life, have paused outside my cubicle and are cackling at me.

'Look at *her*,' one hisses to the other. Instinctively I pull my towel around me, because I am ashamed in a way that deflates me and leaves me feeling like them – like a pre-teen who dislikes herself again, despite the years that have elapsed since then.

Anyway, the girls are on their way out, since they've finished their swim, and I'm only beginning mine. My horrible body and I pad outside to the edge of the water. The pool has a stainless-steel bottom, and it glitters in the low sun. I take to the shimmering blue and I cut a slow length. It has been hot today, but now the temperature is cooling. I swim in the open water, not in the lanes, because I'm slow and choppy, and I like to hang from the lip of the pool while I catch my breath. From here, I can watch the swimmers who have finished their exercise and are now sitting in the last warmth of the evening sun.

There is a couple in their seventies, the man in the water and the woman waiting for him on a bench, minding the bags and towels. He splashes about gently, with great care, and when he is finished, she helps him out of the water. He seems to be suffering from a degenerative illness of some kind and she seems practised at assisting him out of the water, into the embrace of a towel. I look away, having realised that they are not choosing to make this display of tenderness in public view at the side of the pool. They do it out of necessity (changing rooms here being gendered), and out of love, which is their business and not mine.

A reminder that this is a city of nine million people, and I am just one of them.

Another few metres and my mind continues to wander. Here in the water, I can feel far removed from the city itself. I float on my back for a second and see nothing but sky and some trees at the edge of my vision. In the water, I forget the commute that brought me here, the petty indignities of workplace politics, the weight of my swimming gear in the tote bag on my shoulder all day. It's beautiful here and I can forget that the city, or this city at least, is a place that doesn't always allow for the presence of beauty.

For many who live here, London is not defined by its prettiness in the way some other cities are. There are sweet streets of Victorian terraces, pleasant vistas, the wide blue swath of the Thames. From high up on certain vantage points, the city's sprawl can even be breathtaking. But for many who commute through ugly train stations and work in unremarkable buildings, the presiding aesthetic quality of daily life here can be a kind of drabness. A friend of mine, Daniel, once reflected that Londonphilia must be a kind of psychosis. He was making this point when looking back at photos he'd taken of London during his time living here, some years after leaving for Paris – photos he'd tried to show to foreign friends as proof of the city's beauty. They were all grim: rainy junctions at night, or the brimming grey sludge of the Thames.

I think what this means is that you have to work a little harder for the moments of beauty. They are there, in the fabric of the city, where the ancient Roman walls are still visible through skyscrapers, and rivers burble underneath tarmac. The chaotic tangle of centuries of architecture jutting up against each other, with the city as palimpsest beneath it all.

The American urban planner Kevin Lynch wrote that a city is 'a thing perceived only in the course of long spans of time'. His work in the 1950s and 1960s opened up new ways of thinking about cities, and his most influential book, *The Image of the City*, was the product of a five-year study in how people perceive the cities they live in. What he found was that we use the built environment – streets, walls, districts, monuments – to form a mental map of the place where we live. But in his introduction to the book, Lynch also made the point that 'people and their activities, are as important as the stationary physical parts' when it comes to how we experience and make sense of a city.

The lido is architecturally beautiful. The water itself is pleasant. The feeling of relief, of shutting the door on a hectic day, is wonderful. But maybe what I like most about the lido is being in my body here, among other bodies. All day the sight of other people in the city can feel like an affront, a reason to be on the defence. Here it comes, like a balm on chapped skin.

Another length, and my arms begin to ache. I pull myself out of the water and take a seat on the tiered stone steps. Nearby is a woman in her fifties, legs outstretched on a greying white towel, a *Financial Times* beside her and some work documents in one hand. A navy one-piece, the unshowy type made for real swimming, with white piping along the sides, lies next to her on the warm concrete. She combs her silver bob with purpose while leafing through the paper. Her quiet purpose, the pleasure she takes in being by herself, appears like an answer to the questions that dogged me during my twenties. Am I spending my time in the right way? Am I moving in the wrong direction? Is my body wrong somehow? It is so easy to deflect these questions on average days in the city where a busy schedule means I have neither the time nor the inclination to confront the reality of myself.

Here, though, there is a way. A window left ajar, a little fresh air that starts to circulate in a stuffy room.

FIELD NOTES
SUMMER

On the Central Line, around Marble Arch
Twenty degrees out. Warmer underground. The woman one row along is in a furry hat, a minidress, leopard-print sandals and a furry gilet, in a different colour fur from the hat.

Clapham Common
Two slim, tanned joggers argue in Spanish. The blonde woman, in leggings so tight they look as though they have been moulded to her body in liquid plastic, points at her running watch and then gives the other a rude gesture with her fingertips. He frowns, shakes his head and then jogs directly away from her.

Regent's Park
The world's most bored thirteen-year-old trails after his grandparents in the rose garden, hood up and arms folded as they gesture with Nordic poles to one flowering bush after another.

Marylebone High Street

Three taxi drivers, lined up beside their black cabs, waiting for potential fares to exit from the nearby supermarket. It's a dead afternoon. The three drivers are different ages, different builds and demeanours, but they seem to be variations on a theme. One in a hoodie, one in a sleeveless down body-warmer over a t-shirt, one in a polo shirt that looks a little sticky with sweat.

Great Portland Street

A woman in a sundress standing in the shade outside a salad bar, fanning herself idly with a straw sun hat. Around its broad brim, in cursive script: *Living my best life.*

Camden High Street, match day

A lone saxophonist in baseball cap, terracotta-coloured chinos and a short-sleeved shirt playing 'Three Lions' on the pavement, to the delight of the England fans in the pub garden behind him.

Bermondsey beer mile

A group of ebullient women attending a fancy-dress birthday party with the theme of the letter G: I count a gnome, a goat, a guide, a Greek goddess, George Michael, Groovy Chick, two grannies and Gordon Ramsay among their number.

Kentish Town

Three teenage boys, all in high-contrast black and white and Nike trainers, waiting at the traffic lights. In the opposite direction: a tall, wiry metalhead in his fifties, skinny legs in tight denim, wild crop of black hair hanging past his shoulders. The boys jostle each other with glee, pointing at him. One whispers 'weirdo' under his breath as the lights change.

Drummond Street

An older woman in a cream headscarf and an ornate red and gold patterned silk dupatta around her shoulders, video-chatting with friends as she dances at the street party.

Camden High Street

An elderly gentleman in baggy shorts and a holey t-shirt, who has stopped on his bike outside the old bank building. He examines his hair in the reflective surface of the window, licks one hand and slicks his white cowlick back off his forehead a few times. When this doesn't work, he pulls a small plastic comb from his pocket and uses that to finish the job.

Portland Place

A train of neatly dressed school children being escorted to the park. Two teachers lead the way in hi-vis vests over blue chambray; at the rear is the parent-steward, a man in aviator sunglasses and an incongruously fine Italian suit.

St John's Wood
Two very beautiful, very well-put-together young women, both with long dark wavy hair. One photographing, one posing. The posing girl knows her angles, stands with one foot on the kerb to cut a dramatic silhouette in denim shorts and a white crop-top, swinging a monogrammed Dior saddle bag. The photographing friend, in bottle-green leather coat and Air Max sneakers, knows about angles, too, crouching down to get the magnolia and the curved Victorian terrace in the background.

Outside the pub in Cosmo Place, Bloomsbury
Two friends – balding, middle-aged, cheeks rosy from recent sunshine – sitting underneath the awning with their pints, in t-shirts, shorts and tennis shoes soaked through by the afternoon's torrential rain.

Mare Street
Woman in a long blue gingham dress and Jackie O sunglasses laughing to herself, trying to hide her private mirth and failing.

Highgate Hill
A smartly dressed man, nice striped shirt tucked into chino shorts with a belt, carrying a large sign that makes him an endless mystery to me. On one side it is clearly a pilfered roadworks sign, on the other the words 'have the day off' are sloppily painted in primary colours. He carries the cumbersome sign with some care up Highgate Hill.

Waterloo

A muscular man with impressive shoulders wearing a tight black t-shirt and big over-ear headphones, gliding gloriously around Waterloo Roundabout on his e-scooter, heading for the bridge.

The east wing of the National Gallery

A troop of little girls and two accompanying mothers, all of them dressed in pastel cardigans and summery skirts and t-shirts, practical walking shoes and tiny knapsacks. They exit a room in single file.

'Well,' one mother declares. 'We know when we've been told off, don't we, girls?'

4. Walking

There is a certain activity peculiar to city life that I privately refer to as Going Time. In normal day-to-day life, it is impossible to escape Going Time. It is all the time I spend in transit, or waiting, or moving. At a bus stop, my laptop heavy in the tote bag on my shoulder. Walking through Soho after work, weaving in and out of clumps of advertising executives and film people clutching their clammy pints on the pavement. In a dark pub awaiting the arrival of a friend – trying not to watch the door for her entrance, trying to focus on my book. On the Tube home, head resting on the glass, wedged next to a stranger in a puffy black coat. Queuing for the self-service checkout in Sainsbury's, a chorus of beeps echoing while I'm faintly aware of the black soot in my nostrils from the journey underground. All of this is Going Time. I am always on my way somewhere, even when I am not moving.

Going Time is tiring. It adds up easily, and I often fail to take it into account when making plans. But it's also fruitful. It's when I have ideas, desires. I plan for the future and process my past. I overhear the conversations of people beside me. I observe. I react. In doing so, I leave myself open, too. Because I don't have a choice: I am a human in the world, and I have chosen to live here in this way.

Going Time is lonely, because it is time spent alone in public. Yet I never feel lonely. I feel most myself, I think, seated alone in a pub with a book – waiting. Listening to the two men beside me talk about the shuttered pub they want to buy together in the Cotswolds, how they'll turn it into a rural retreat for bankers from the City. I listen, and hope they don't notice me or intrude on my solitude. Going Time is a time for encounters that can occur without intrusion. I don't want to be disturbed, because being disturbed means that I have been seen. I prefer to be the one doing the seeing.

* * *

I am twenty-one. I stand up from my desk at 8 p.m., philosophy essay finally complete, and put my parka on. I start walking down the hill to meet my boyfriend and our friends on a grassy slope. It has been snowing all day – rare enough in Dublin that there is a sense of holiday mayhem in the night air – and we are going to go sledding. It is a short walk, fifteen minutes or so, but the beer I drank earlier while editing my essay means I need a wee. I stop into the pub beside the slope, the place my family has always gone for last-minute fish-and-chip dinners over the years, and beeline for the toilet.

In the cubicle, I hear a shuffling noise. On the periphery of my vision a shadow passes. I look up, and over the top of the cubicle divider, a man's face is visible. He holds a phone in one hand, and I hear the artificial click of the phone's camera. I swear in fright, standing up and rearranging my heavy coat around me. I throw open the door and he is already gone. A woman enters through the doors of the toilets, a look of confusion on her face.

'Sorry,' I say. My breathing is heavy in my voice. 'Did you just see a man coming out of here?'

'Oh, yes,' she replies. 'He walked right into me! I think he went into the wrong toilets.'

I'm already heading for the door. 'No, he didn't,' I say over my shoulder.

Back in the pub's lounge, I flag down a waitress and tell her what happened. She takes my arm and a hard, angry look comes over her face. This has happened before, she says, and instructs the other staff to see if he is still here. I am a little shaky. She sits me down and brings me a gin and tonic – heavy on the gin – while she calls the police. I call my boyfriend, who arrives in minutes, looking for someone to fight.

I talk to the police, but nothing ever happens. My boyfriend holds me on the sofa while I cry. I am angry. I am twenty-one, and so the world is full of men who think that looking at me offers them some part of me to own. That by looking at me, they can have access to some part of me I would never give them with consent. I am twenty-one, and a woman, and now all the streets around my home feel dangerous. All the men I know seem potentially untrustworthy. I am a twenty-one-year-old woman who is constantly reminded that she is not in charge of how she is received in the world, whatever she does. Male sexual entitlement permeates everything as soon as I leave the house – the way I can walk on the streets or empty my bladder. I am twenty-one years old, and as the winter gives way to spring, in my final year of university, I worry that this anger will never go away.

Then I am twenty-two. It is summer. After university I move to New York to work in an East Village thrift store and intern at a fashion magazine. I live with the same boyfriend in the basement of a brownstone on Carlton Avenue in Prospect Heights. I work every single day that summer. There are no days off. I walk up Carlton Avenue in the morning heat and take the Q train to Manhattan. One day when my shift ends early, I take the train across town to meet my boyfriend near his work at the United Nations. I am wearing a cream sundress I bought in the thrift store – it's a piece of merchandise from the New Orleans Jazz Festival and has little dragonflies on it, with the name of the festival written on the wings. I sit on the moulded plastic bench and across from me, an unstable man lies down on the opposite bench to look up my skirt. I stand up and hold my skirt with one hand, the subway pole with the other. I get off a stop early.

Time passes. I begin to think the city is curing me. It must, because if I want to live here and work this much, I need to be capable of being alone, being looked at as I move around the city. I wonder if a stronger woman would be less bothered by all of this, and then I decide that I can just be a stronger woman, if I want to be. There are new kinds of Going Time that I haven't yet experienced, never having lived somewhere like this before. I work constantly, drinking huge amounts of iced coffee that sloshes caffeine through my system like pure adrenaline. After work I go to new addresses to meet my friends in parks and dive bars and DIY venues in breach of every possible fire safety regulation. I queue for the toilet in one, the can of PBR beer turning warm in my hand. In the cubicle, I check the walls and floors like I have done in every public toilet I have used since December the previous year. The toilet cubicle is made of plywood and I could probably knock it down with a little kick of my foot. Through the wall I can hear two people having sex, or almost, in the next one. If I am looking for a safe, private space to pee in, this is not it. But my bladder is full. I can be anxious and fearful, I think to myself, or I can just do this anyway.

I walk home alone at night, feeling invincible. I find that I have a blind, arrogant confidence that I will be safe anywhere.

I can always just run, can't I? Maybe, when it came to it, my speed would surprise me. I walk for hours, entranced by New York's blocky pattern of streets, from the Time-Life Building where I intern on Sixth Avenue, past the stage door of Radio City where an actor in ghoulish green make-up smokes a cigarette on his lunch break, his eyes lingering on me. One night I fall over and cut my knee – that summer I am always falling over in my impractical sandals, the thin skin on my bare knees always so ready to burst open – and walk to the 24-hour drugstore for plasters. Outside I wipe the blood from my knee with a tissue while two policemen tell me, in firm voices, to move away from the building, because there is an armed siege going on in the apartment above it. I dye the ends of my long hair blue and in the East Village thrift store where I work, I watch a group of intimidatingly cool fifteen-year-old skaters come in. The girl throws a Harley-Davidson t-shirt on the counter and pays for it; she is beautiful and nonchalant and while I'm wrapping it up for her, she looks me in the eye with a confidence I never had as a teenager.

'Your hair is fucking sick,' she says, and for the rest of the day I buzz with the glee of having impressed one of the popular kids.

I barely sleep. In the early mornings and the late evenings, I walk the landlady's dog, my headphones in, around the block. The dog is a Puli, a kind of Hungarian sheepdog with thick curly fur that can coil into dreadlocks, and she gets a lot of attention on our walks.

'Obama's dog!' a little white girl shouts, pointing at Tsipi and then grabbing a fistful of her fur like she is a stuffed toy.

I am walking by the basketball court, thinking of the pizza I'm going to pick up for dinner. There is a commotion in front of me, and a group of people who had previously been static suddenly scatter. There are two men, one with a video camera, and three made-up girls in short denim shorts and high heels. The dog and I have interrupted a low-budget music video shoot.

'Let's do it again,' the man beside the cameraman sighs, jabbing a thumb in my direction. 'From the top. The dog was in that shot.'

I must be cured now, I think. There is no fear or anxiety left in me. There is only a hunger for experience, for newness. I can go anywhere – can walk across the Brooklyn Bridge, the lights of the city spread out and glittering like glass in a wound – and everything I do is ripe with meaning. New York is a filmset, and here I am, a bit-part actor with no lines, ready and willing to become another cliché.

On the subway to my magazine internship I watch a stream of commuters trickle over to the last remaining empty seat, then recoil as they notice the stain on it. Their faces are all hardened in the same way. I am faintly aware that I am twenty-two and particularly porous to the universe. Everything is bright and intense and I will not always feel this open.

The rain in New York is like nothing I've seen before. It's like an on/off switch, the skies opening. Biblical. I am always in open-toed shoes, the whole summer long. When the rain comes, it leaves tidemarks on my feet. I stand under shop awnings and wait for it to pass. The awnings shake under the pelting. The rain is violent. The dog hates it. When I get home from my walks my skin is covered in a thin layer of the city's grime, and I am disgusted as I wipe it off with soap and cotton wool, but also a little enthralled. This is New York, I think, touching the grey dirt with my finger. Even this counts.

September comes and I pack my things. I hand the keys back to the landlady and say goodbye to Tsipi. I have my boyfriend take a final photo of myself sitting on the stoop. This bit – leaving – is temporary, I tell myself. I feel certain I will be back to New York, because my life is an open network of many different wires, all of which can connect if I want them to. I think of electrical boxes on the street, doors open, all their coloured cables hanging out. But the moment the plane takes off, I am aware that the New York chapter is over, regardless of whatever happens in the future. I have a connection to make in London, the last flight of the day home to Dublin, and since the first leg is delayed, I begin to worry pointlessly that I won't make it and will be stranded in Heathrow overnight. As we come in to land, the flight attendant sitting on the fold-out seat nearby reassures me that this won't happen, and I go back to my thoughts about New York. That was the summer I was twenty-two, I think, and as the plane hits the tarmac in London I realise I am crying. All of it is coming out at once. The flight attendant, bless him, leans over and pats my forearm sweetly.

'Really,' he says with kindness. 'I promise you won't miss your connection.'

I just nod blankly at him.

Back home, preparing to move to London for a masters, I break up with the boyfriend – over the summer, the fact that he never came to the police station with me in December weighs heavier and heavier on me, and also, I begin to find that our politics are not aligned, and also, I am not in love with him. As time passes, I find that I do not stay cured. New York has a half-life and it begins to leave my system. Iced coffee starts to make me panicky and nauseous, rather than euphoric. It's not all bad, though: the skin on my knees thickens, and over the years I switch to wearing more practical shoes. I start to become a different person. I will start to find that I am always doing this. I am filled with different fears and anxieties, and as I get older the panacea of new experience is not always enough to push me through them. I am still cautious of public toilets, though I do use them, because the alternative is never going anywhere. I keep walking, but the porousness within me has changed. I am open, but I am also wary sometimes. It's a balance that I try to maintain, and I often remember the person I was during the summer in New York when I am feeling lost or confused or hurt by the city where I live now. Lonely, maybe. I cannot go back to her, and sometimes I envy her that wilful freedom and blind confidence. It couldn't last. It was a trick of the light, a window that couldn't stay open if I was to grow. But I can remember the part of myself that I left on a stoop in Brooklyn.

* * *

In London, for the first time in my life nobody knew where I was supposed to be at any given hour of the day. Nobody expected me home for dinner, would panic if I didn't show up. I had classes and I had friends, and soon I had a job, but my earliest impressions of London were the sensation of being unmoored from that which had once kept me grounded. It felt exciting, and it also felt dangerous.

Around that time, in the early 2010s, discussion around sexism and privilege began to feature more prominently than ever before in conversation. Coming as it did from debate among broadsheet columnists and bloggers, who themselves tended to be white, educated and middle-class, it would often home in on the problems and indignities faced by young, educated white women. Women like me. It was easy, then, for me to feel that the experience of walking down the street as a young woman was fraught, vexed, in a way that nothing else could be.

Living here in the belly of a new anonymity, I began to feel both more and less on display. In the city where I'd grown up, it was normal to bump into two, four or ten people you knew well on any excursion outside the home. Here, the art college I attended was a colosseum of style I could barely compete in, and everything else in the city was new and blank. I started to dress in baggier clothing: loose, pyjama-like trousers and men's t-shirts. A huge woollen jumper six sizes too big over everything. A shapeless camel coat. Combat boots, or cheap white sneakers, sometimes soft leather jazz shoes not made for city streets and commuting. They made me feel as though I was dancing through the city, its concrete the sprung floor of the practice studio.

I could not have told you then what I was doing with the baggy clothes, other than that I was learning I did not owe anything to the anonymous men with whom I shared a city, I didn't owe them a smile or a pretty outfit. I thought that by making myself nondescript, a void, I was reclaiming some space or getting the upper hand.

I think now what I was doing was pretending there wasn't a problem. I was refusing to confront the reality of my own body; I was denying it space. This isn't to say I should have been wearing more feminine or more revealing clothing. There is no correct or incorrect way for any woman to dress herself. But I was not comfortable in myself. I wouldn't be for years. I was still vain then, and wanted very badly to be told I was beautiful or glamorous or interesting – my idea of my selfhood rested on how others saw me, rather than how I saw myself. But I was busy making myself invisible. I think that became an important method of dressing, and it's something I continue to reach for from time to time.

Now, I like to have the option of feeling invisible. I like that I can dress a certain way and feel like I am part of the background of the city. This is not to say that how I dress is responsible for any harassment or violence I might experience on the street. One way the conversation around women's safety has progressed since I first moved here is that there is a greater understanding that male violence and harassment are due to the man perpetrating them, and not the woman and what she might be wearing. But I've learned that a cultivated invisibility can be useful in other ways. It's jarring sometimes to realise that I too am being watched – by CCTV, by individuals, by societal expectations about who I am, as a woman, a white person, someone with particular privileges. These privileges can dictate everything about how I'm treated in any given location. Walking through the city, I slip into a Mayfair gallery to look at an exhibition of Japanese ceramics; I'm regarded as harmless by the attendant in her expensive shoes. I am meeting a friend at a nice restaurant and because I am early, I sit at the bar. The bartender takes one look at me, serves me a drink, and goes back to paying attention to the well-dressed, moneyed couple beside me. I am unimportant here. In designer boutiques, so long as I'm dressed nicely, staff will gladly let me browse. They might even think I want to buy something. On quiet streets in Chelsea or Belgravia, I'm viewed as a lost tourist or maybe even a resident, rather than as an outsider or a threat. I can usually, I've noticed, persuade most businesses to let me use the customers-only toilet.

Dressing with anonymity or invisibility in mind can help smooth these processes for me. But it's not purely a question of my clothes. I can control my clothes, after all – I can wear what I want and notice how I am treated differently by the city as a result. To a certain extent, the reason I'm viewed as harmless or part of the background is dependent on my race, my size, my class presentation and my able body. Physically, I am broadly in line with the kind of person who might spend money in the Yohji Yamamoto boutique, or who might be a lost tourist on a Belgravia backstreet. While a Black shopper may experience racial profiling in a department store, the world tends to turn a blind eye to me, and the city allows me to browse and wander and observe in relative peace.

As a Londoner, I also benefit from the fact that London was once the seat of empire – despite the fact that I am Irish and that historically, Ireland and Irish people were oppressed by the British Empire. Today, London is a rich city full of economic opportunity, world-class culture and interesting curiosities partly because of the violence and theft committed by the British Empire all over the world for centuries. The legacy of this violence is visible all through the fabric of the city, in its monuments to military leaders, in the names of its streets. I benefit from this in the way that all Londoners can and do, but more so because I am white. If I am safe here, I know I should be asking: Whose safety is compromised on my behalf? Who is not safe?

These same inequalities also carve the city up, leaving wide swaths on the map where I might never have reason to go. The positive attributes of urban life are not distributed equally through the territory. They congregate in wealthier neighbourhoods. But I would be lying if I said I don't use these benefits to my advantage often – wandering into the grounds of apartment complexes to have a closer look at the architecture, pretending to be lost if anyone asks me what I'm doing. I think all white people everywhere take advantage of whiteness, whether we are aware of doing so or not; we do it without even questioning how we benefit from the very racism that makes it difficult for others to move with this same freedom.

I like Going Time so much because it centres me as an observer. It turns downtime into something that feels stimulating and unique to city life and in doing so, it becomes easy for me to feel like an objective onlooker. But I know there is no such thing as an objective onlooker – I bring to my looking all of my own identities and biases, my accumulated experiences as an able-bodied and inconspicuous white woman, living in cities that were built for people like me.

There can never be real objectivity while observing a city like London, where everywhere you turn there are barriers to movement that relate to class, race and money. When I move around this city, I try to bear that in mind.

AN ANONYMOUS MEMBER OF A DISTINGUISHED LONDON CLUB

How long have you been a member of your club?

Since 2013. So, whatever that is. Eight years.

What was it that made you want to join a club?

I was appointed director of an institute that relies on face-to-face contacts, building networks. And I needed somewhere to do that in London. You can't keep asking people to come to Oxford. Otherwise it was sort of going into people's offices – not always helpful. Why this club? Because there was a guy who was on the advisory board, and he was at the club. And thirdly, I always liked the look of it, because it's just around the corner from the British Academy, where I'm a member.

It is a very handsome building as well.

Mmm. Lovely gardens.

Do you remember how you felt the first time you went as a member?

Since I'd been there a few times [as a guest], I just made sure I was dressed appropriately.

What did that mean?

A tie. A suit.

So if you hadn't been wearing a tie and a suit, you would not have gained entry.

They will provide you with a tie and jacket if needed. And that has happened once or twice.

When you're in the area and didn't expect to be stopping in?

Guests who didn't believe me when I said the club really does require a tie and a jacket.

Was the formal dress code something that appealed to you in choosing a club?

It's not terribly important one way or another. There's a sort of a formality to it all that starts from the front door and goes all the way through the organisation. But it's a kind of a formality of mutual recognition, rather than a formality for formality's sake.

Is that kind of formality part of your career as well?

I'm an academic. Going around Oxford colleges, you don't have to wear jackets and ties and things like that. Maybe you used to, but well before my time.

So the club is a departure from your daily dress code.

Yeah, although going around, having meetings with the key people I need to meet, I would dress well. If you're going to meet a CEO of a major corporation, you dress well. Tie, jacket.

Do you have any interest in clothing of your own?

Growing up my mother always said I had expensive taste. Then again, she really didn't like spending money. I suppose the style police are my wife and my son – my son dresses really well. I like a good suit, yeah. Who wouldn't?

Has being a member of your club motivated you to purchase more suits than you would have otherwise?

No. It's all about the business, the job. To put it in context, you go into the dining room, which is what the club's all about at lunchtime. And basically, there you see thirty-year-olds through to ninety-year-olds. The younger they are, the better dressed they are. The older they are, the more likely they are to be wearing the same thing they've worn for twenty years. So in that sense: yeah, I wouldn't go in there dressed like a ninety-year-old.

This is a club that prides itself on being one of the first to open up to women. I've never had a sense of what their dress code is.

I think women's dress codes tend to use terminology that can be difficult to interpret.

Is that right? Obviously they dress well. Sometimes it appears to me that women are more self-conscious about what they're wearing in the club. I think generally, they dress better than men.

With a suit, there are only so many permutations. When I've spoken to CEOs about what they wear, they say there are huge benefits to having one thing that you wear - a suit - that you can wear all the time, since you don't have to make any additional decisions about it.

So, if I'm going to a very important meeting, I'll wear a blue suit, white shirt, blue tie. I'm very conscious of what that signifies. If I'm in London, seeing people I know, I'll be less self-conscious. The blue suit might not get a chance to make it down there.

When you say you're conscious of what it signifies, what does the blue suit signify?

A blue expensive suit is a marker of – you can afford it, but equally there's a sense of being sharp. Being sharp is an important signifier.

5. On Coldharbour Lane

A few summers ago I was walking to the train station to go meet someone about a job. I was late. I was wearing a white t-shirt and the afternoon was hot: I was trying to walk slowly so as not to sweat, but fast enough that I might actually make my train and not be late.

I was nearing the final corner when a woman came out onto her flat balcony a few metres to my left, two storeys up. She caught my eye immediately. She was wearing quite an exciting dress, a traditional Spanish or South American style in a pink and green print – far too fancy for the hour. A dress for dancing. She must be going somewhere nice, I thought.

'You,' she shouted down at me. 'Come up here and zip me up please.'

In the space of seconds, thoughts raced through my head: Could I go into this stranger's house? What were the risks?

What would my mother say about me entering a stranger's home like this? But also – what was the opportunity cost if I did not? What would I learn from doing it? Would she tell me where the dress came from, or where she was going to wear it? Would there be a good story behind it, one I could take and form into a story of my own to tell and retell? And also, what would her flat smell like? Would it be messy, repulsive to a stranger? Would the dress fit her perfectly, or would I have to pull the two sides of the fabric tight over this stranger's back – her skin probably sweaty like mine in the heat – to get the zipper up? Would I have to make a joke about this, to break the tension? It was so intimate even to think about. Would I say, 'OK, take a deep breath,' and then, when I'd managed to get the zipper all the way up, pat her neatly on the back and say, 'Perfect'?

She waved a hand at me. She was a lot older than me, maybe twice my age.

'Come on,' she called. 'I can't do it alone. Please!'

I shook my head. 'I've got a train to catch,' I called up, which was the truth and also a sentence I do like having the chance to utter. I heard her groan, like I was the fifth person to let her down that day. I shrugged an apology and kept walking to the station.

I made the train, seconds to spare. But I spent the rest of the day thinking about it. This was the opportunity cost – a little puddle of regret that would not drain away that afternoon. Actually, it would not drain away for years. I am still stepping into it now, long after I moved out of that neighbourhood. I find myself awake in the middle of the night, thinking about it. I wonder if she ever got the dress zipped up. I wonder if my life would have been different in any way, had I helped her zip it up. If I had been a different person I would've done it, missed my train, not cared about the job interview. I didn't get the job anyway. I should've just told her to come down to the street, I realise, and to hurry up, but now it's a little bit late for that.

6. In Shoreditch

On a morning's commute from my home to the fringes of
the City, I see the following: a father and two children on
a bicycle built for three, pedalling furiously up the hill to
school. A lone navy ballet flat fallen onto the train tracks. I
see a man in an Hermès tie who shoulders onto the carriage
ahead of me, then unfurls his newspaper in such a way that
the passengers around him are forced to shrink away. I see a
woman who wraps one arm around the pole, carefully main-
taining her balance as she lifts one foot out of her high heel
and rubs the heel against her other ankle. I see a carriage full
of people who would rather be elsewhere and who are using
their faces to communicate this – the cold, obliviousness
that city dwellers use as a kind of self-defence. I see a man
with a cello – *a cello, in rush hour* – who manoeuvres apologeti-
cally into the space of four people, all of whom disembark at

King's Cross. This is a place far from pleasure. Young and old, but mostly in the middle, that segment of society whose daily lives are given over to wage-earning and who all, in order to do so, must for some reason travel on this screeching, packed sardine can.

I myself disembark at Old Street, and I ride the escalator out of the bowels of the underground system and up to street level. From the moment I step off the Tube until I reach my office I am moving in a constant flow of people, like a blurry time-lapse segment from the documentary *Koyaanisqatsi*. Old Street rush hour on the pavements is mainly made up of well-dressed working people, women who pay close attention to trends in day dresses and flat shoes, and good-looking men in very clean streetwear. Tailoring would not be appropriate here. That's for a little further south, in the City. Here, status and power and money are communicated differently, thanks to the area's links to tech, fashion and the endlessly shifting zeitgeist of cultural capital.

It is pleasing to me to notice the codes of the fashion girls around here – the leopard-print midi skirt, the suede mules, the clean white sneakers with the glowing neon letter embossed on each one. It's like learning a language from a textbook in a classroom, then getting the opportunity to put it into practice. It is also pleasing for me to embed the codes into my own outfit. There is a strange thrill in first noticing the cliché in the wild, and then allowing yourself to become that cliché, too.

What this means is that by the time I get to my office, I've seen eight different outfits that I'd like to wear. I am firing up eBay on my phone as I make a cup of tea in the kitchen. I am saving searches for *leopard print midi* and *vintage prairie dress* and *brown leather coat* and *black patent trousers*. I am also curious about Noah sweatshirts, Aimé Leon Dore hats and Albam smock jackets, because they seem expensive and prestigious, and knowing just how expensive and prestigious they are will allow me to modulate my opinions of the men who wear them.

I am unsure if *black patent trousers* will make me better at my job, but they might impart a bit of confidence, along with the kind of blissful, serotonin-laden high I get when I buy something that ticks a particular box for me. There is an insistent little voice at the back of my head that says, so yes, maybe these trousers will change your life. Certainly, there are colleagues in the kitchen with me, also making tea, who seem to be walking with a particular confidence in their own nice outfits. Here is more evidence, I note, that *black patent trousers* will make it easier to give a third of my life to this office.

Anyway, I make my tea and turn on my laptop and stop thinking about the life-changing power of black patent trousers for an hour or two. I go to a meeting where a male colleague is wearing a tall, slouching beanie hat. Now I'm thinking about hats, and how this man wears one so that the rest of us know something about him – that he is cool, worldly, knowing. He has done his homework, this man, and so we should take his opinions and his credentials seriously. I don't necessarily need proof that he is good at his job, because he has this noteworthy hat. I can know this and still be taken in by it. The same way I add extra grip to my handshake when I am introduced to an older man in a suit. I know that his suit is just an outfit, that his age and appearance don't make him stronger or more powerful than me, and yet I end up acting as if it does.

At lunchtime I feel compelled to leave the office, even when I have a pre-packed lunch of leftovers and a pile of work to get through. I need the chance to breathe, to wander around Liverpool Street and see if anything unexpected is happening. Also, I need to buy myself a tiny treat as a reward for getting through half the day. I think about these small trade-offs I constantly make for myself as I walk to the market in Spitalfields. There is a branch of mental mathematics that deals with time, money and how I spend them both, and which I value most. Some days I am better at doing these sums than others.

When I first moved to London I worried so much about work, about money, about what would happen if I could find neither, about how that would lead to my leaving here. I was right to worry about the difficulty of securing all of it. Without a source of passive income, working is always necessary if you are to live in the city. I didn't have time to stop and think about what you trade when you go to work: your time and energy, yes, but also a part of yourself. Work makes you into something, someone who buys Hermès ties or slouching beanie hats, or who is rude to her fellow commuters every morning. It shapes what you think of as acceptable and unacceptable, in clothing and in social mores.

I buy myself a cookie. Dark chocolate chip and sea salt, in a greasy paper bag. The market is covered and when I emerge, I am surprised to find it has started to rain heavily. I shove the cookie into the deep pocket of my coat, which is sometimes called a trench coat and sometimes called a mackintosh. I've been calling it my raincoat recently, since I learned that Leonard Cohen's 'Famous Blue Raincoat' wasn't a waterproofed anorak. It was an old Burberry mac much like my own. It makes sense to me; a raincoat, I think, is the most cinematic of items in a wardrobe. It feels like an insignia of sorts for the person who wears it, coming into the office from the rain, hanging it up. The puddle dripping underneath the coat rack becomes an extension of the wearer.

Maybe it is the quintessential London garment. It certainly could be for me. I moved to London to pursue a career, to live my life, to find who I was or should be and all that. But I also moved because I thought that I could probably find a great second-hand Burberry mac here, and once I did, I would have places to wear it. I found one. Mine is olive green and long, and belted at the neat, high waist. It's the best-constructed garment I've ever owned. I feel like a spy when I wear it, except that of course a spy would never dress so conspicuously spy-like. Sometimes, wearing it in late autumn, walking through leaves around Bloomsbury squares, passing through Senate House or running up the stairs at the Brunswick Centre at just the right time of day, I can feel it: the cinematic quality of my own life, barely sensible most of the time, suddenly pools all around me like oil coming up through the ground.

You can be happy in a city like London without the need for any specific item of clothing. There is no weather or no activity unique to urban life that creates a real necessity for, say, waterproof boots or a functional jacket. An umbrella is a good idea, though I've known many who seem quite content to go without. But a raincoat – I'm thinking of a mackintosh or trench coat rather than the more sturdy, hardy outdoors garments – can feel like a necessity here.

I wait for the pedestrian lights to change on Bishopsgate and as I do, two men amble slowly in my direction. They are deep in conversation, one carrying a battered sports bag and the other clutching a can of beer. They are dressed at odds with everyone else on the street; I think that if the buildings that line this street had their way, with their rampant desire for more profit, these men would not be here at all. The argument being that they don't contribute to the economy the way I do with my day of waged work, the expensive cookie in my coat pocket. If they must be here, the city seems to say, the least you can do is not look at them. That's what everyone else at the traffic lights does as the two men walk by.

Clothes can feel so silly at times, so trivial. There are real and tangible problems in the world. There is injustice everywhere I turn, especially in the city, which seems to breed a very specific kind of injustice and inequality. Should I apologise for looking so much at the surface when there are such problems lying beneath? I don't know if I can help it. It would require me to turn away from so much of the outside world, and I'm not sure if I know how to do that.

In the office I hang up my coat and take my seat. Now I am thinking of a job interview I did once, when I was very green, at a magazine where I thought I wanted to work. I was new to London and did not know how I was supposed to dress for such things. There seemed to be a rulebook, I was realising, but I was not sure where to get a copy of it. Instead I went to the second-hand shop I liked in Stepney Green and bought a canary-yellow silk blazer. I wore it over a short black shift dress and with the Swedish clogs I wore with everything back then.

The woman interviewing me was high-powered and lovely. She wore a proper suit but one with a casual elegance that I thought of as European – an open-necked silk shirt, a thin gold chain at her breastbone. Her hair was loose and tucked behind her ear. I sat neatly, my legs crossed at the ankle, my hands in my lap, and answered her questions expansively.

I did not get the job. I found out the next day, while I was studying in the college library. That stupid yellow jacket, I thought. It was much easier to disavow an item of clothing than it was my own personality.

I continued to wear the yellow jacket. I still wear it now. Over the years, it became less risky to have a person-ality in the workplace. You get a little bit older and people tend to understand you better. It feels like there is less of a requirement to fit a certain mould, and when you develop skills of your own, less rides on your appearance. Ever since that interview long ago, though, I have had a deep, gnawing need never to feel inadequate or embarrassed in another one ever again, and this means I rely on certain items of clothing. I outsource some of the labour involved in being palatable, presentable, to my wardrobe. The magic of clothing, I think, as I sit at my desk and glance back at my coat on its hook. A weapon I can carry in my arsenal, so I have a little less work to do myself.

On the way home, I stop first at a small supermarket to get the ingredients for dinner. This supermarket is chaotic and ramshackle, despite being part of a chain that, in childhood, seemed more solid to me than anything else in society. It is difficult to obtain the ingredients for a full meal in this shop, unless the meal is filled pasta, a pre-made sauce and a cheap bottle of sweet white wine. However it's the only option that doesn't involve a detour, and the minutes that elapse between when I leave the office and when I reach home always feel like the most fleeting and valuable of my whole day.

The queue for the Tube begins above ground, outside the station entrance. It is hard to see how anyone could enjoy this part of the day. It is easy, also, to see how this would drive people out of the city, in search of a simpler routine made of journeys that are less complicated.

With my paltry groceries I join the mass of shuffling hundreds, eyes pointed down towards phone screens or clutched free newspapers. A grey peacoat jostles my arm near the ticket barriers. At ground level, I see desert boots and Derby shoes, the sharp angles of low heels with pointed toes. Through this array of shoes I can see the different lives the Tube passengers have been living all day. Once in the carriage we are stationary and stop shuffling. Backpacks, designer handbags, greying canvas tote bags acquired from conferences and magazine subscriptions. Brand names on sweatshirts, t-shirts printed with stupid jokes, a novelty sock in a cannabis leaf-print peeping from under the cuff of a trouser leg. I know why commuters shut the world out with headphones, books and flashing phone games. The ads on the carriage walls alone are a visual bombardment, a sensory overload. Add in the dense array of messages communicated by the clothing of your fellow travellers and this small segment of everyday life can threaten to overwhelm the senses.

It is a relief to reach my station and join the string of people standing on the escalator. Kentish Town station is plagued by a strong downward gust of wind, and on occasion I've seen hats swept from heads as their owners reach the top. I remove my own and hold it to my chest as I am heaved slowly back up to street level.

Home. I take off my shoes, hang up my coat. I pad around the flat in my socks and put water on the hob to boil. I pull the bobby pins from my hair and lay them on the countertop. Slowly, in this way, I undo the day and return to something more like myself, whether that's a good thing or not.

FIELD NOTES
AUTUMN

Regent's Canal, King's Cross
A slender woman, pensionable age, in a lilac jumper and skinny jeans, single-handedly opening the paddles of the lock to make way for a charming sky-blue boat. Behind her, a man the same age in a grey fleece guides the boat into the lock and secures it with rope.

The undercroft of the Southbank Centre
Two tiny girls on skateboards barely bigger than them, bravely navigating the graffitied slopes in miniature skate shoes and baggy jeans of almost comical proportions.

Holloway Road
A man in a fine grey two-piece suit, worn a little loose. He stamps his cigarette on the wet pavement with his sneakers

before entering the Somali social club at the back of the minicab office.

Waterlow Park, Highgate

'Not everyone likes you, puppy,' a sensible-looking woman in a pink quilted jacket admonishes her black and white sheepdog, who has just jumped, slobbering, into the lap of a girl sitting on a bench.

Hampstead Heath Extension

Two women walking in lockstep, both modestly dressed in the same black skirts and tights. Same neat haircuts. Different running shoes, similar but different practical down-puffer jackets in shades of dark grey.

Trafalgar Square

A man in a red plastic poncho branded with the name of an open-top bus tour company is kneeling on the pavement, affixing fridge magnets shaped like Big Ben and red phone boxes to the walls of his kiosk.

Swain's Lane

The cyclists, usually men, usually in a group, usually all white and ultra slim, pushing themselves up hills. They wear expensive technical clothes – shorts that reveal a layer of padding when they stand up on their pedals, or nylon t-shirts with the name of an investment bank on the back. They pant, heave, spit and sometimes dismount to urinate when they reach the top of the hill, backs straight and hands at their waists. Their watches beep in unison.

At a gallery off Great Eastern Street
A man in black trousers, rolled at the ankles, and a black knit hat, also rolled at its brim. His hands are clasped behind him as he walks from photograph to photograph, nodding to himself.

Regent's Park
A man in scruffy tracksuit bottoms veers off the path and into the mud and pauses, removing his phone from his tracksuit bottom pocket. He looks to the east where the pink terrace of Regency mansions is hidden behind the trees and takes a photo. I can see the screen from where I sit; the picture is purest autumn. Yellow leaves on green grass, the outline of a Labrador in the middle ground, the money and wealth of the big houses barely visible at the edges of the image.

White Cube gallery, Bermondsey
Girl with a neat black bob and neon orange nails wearing a tweed miniskirt, fishnets, Dr. Martens, Louis Vuitton hand-bag, taking photos of the gallery's various concrete angles on her phone.

On the Piccadilly Line
Couple in a combination of outdoor gear and Wimbledon merchandise sitting across from each other. She extends

one foot for him to fasten the adjustable pull cord on her hiking sandal and he does so, then gestures at her to extend her other foot. They both have the tan of healthy pensioners who spend a lot of time outside.

Frith Street

Woman in a thigh-length coat entirely covered in sequins that fade from violet to magenta. Bare legs and cream cowboy boots. Beside her a man in a black and white going-out shirt and very clean tailored jeans.

Frith Street, half an hour later

A tall woman with a voluminous shoulder-length Afro, balayage dip-dyed, wearing a printed silk kimono and high caramel patent heels, heading up the steps to Ronnie Scott's.

7. In Smithfield

I am alone at a table waiting for my friend Aoife who has just told me she'll be an hour – one whole hour – late. It's dark, and I have a copy of the *New Yorker* folded over and held close to the candle on the table, but really it's too dark to read.

The front door opens and my head turns like it's on casters. Of course it's not Aoife. Her train is still somewhere far away. It's two women, dressed fantastically. They breeze into the dark pub in a haze of laughter and sandalwood perfume. The taller one, in a long, printed silk dress, red cowboy boots and a light-blue Afghan coat, is more eye-catching, but her friend is more beautiful, wearing white jeans and a faux leather coat printed to look like snakeskin. They take a seat at the table near me and all of a sudden I don't mind that Aoife is so late and that it's too dark to read my magazine. Now I have something else to take in.

The women haven't seen each other in a while, and as they settle I hear them express incredulity that it has been so long, and also that they have managed to meet at all. They've both been travelling more lately, and one's just started a new job. We've been like ships in the night, the shorter woman says, and I think of the city after dark as the sea, quiet and calm but full of hidden currents. They make jokes and laugh – the taller one slapping the table with the palm of her hand – and their delight at each other is infectious. It makes me giddy enough that I finish my drink without noticing.

When Aoife arrives, she brings the anxiety of her delayed journey with her. It spills out onto the table as she unravels her scarf from around her neck, the story of her late-running meeting and the quotidian drama of a delayed train. I let her at it. She needs to get it out and I know the feeling well. I would like to change the tempo and show Aoife the two women, because they are still captivating – they are now talking to a handsome man who runs the bar, or perhaps the kitchen, and who clearly wants to impress them – but it's pointless, because the energy I spent looking at them, waiting for Aoife, evaporates on Aoife's arrival.

They would have you believe it's near impossible, meeting up with friends in a city like this. The back and forth about finding a date in the diary. The stop-start of the last-minute cancellation, the rescheduling. It feels like a miracle when it does happen, and I'm thankful that Aoife agrees, the way she leans over the table to tell me she's so happy to see me, her glossy hair forming a curtain that blocks my view of the women at the next table. I forget about them and instead tell Aoife about my news, the problems in my writing that I'm working through, the hunt for a place to live. She tells me about the man she was seeing, who has disappeared from her life, and the flat she is thinking of buying, provided she gets the pay rise she's expecting. I go to the toilets, and on my way back I stop at the bar to buy us a round. When I return, Aoife beckons me close to her. For a second I think she is going to say something about the women at the next table. Maybe they have finally caught her eye, now that they have two handsome men sitting with them, one of whom has a small West Highland Terrier on his lap. There is a frisson of intimacy, sexual tension, which trickles over from their table. But Aoife is in her own world. Her view of the night is different. She wants to tell me about something that happened to her last weekend, on another night out in the city. I want to hear what she has to say, so I push her pint glass over towards her and lean in to listen.

* * *

Why do I bother going out? This is a question that occurs to me sometimes on a long bus journey home, looking at my dwindling bank balance on my phone, counting the hours of sleep I'll snatch before the alarm sounds once again to wake me for work. I end up spending so much time arranging things: coordinating diaries, deciding how best to use my free time, making the booking, crossing the city, queueing outside, finding the ATM, trying to get my order in at the bar, trying to hear my friends over the background noise. But on the balance of things, it tends to be worth the effort. Sometimes the night can be fraught or boring, misspent, a waste of my precious time. But more often than not I give in. After all, it is easy to remember why I might want to go out. I have a bank of memories to draw on, a jewellery box of fragments that connect across the city, of things that took place once after dark.

Good music in a dark room. New people, friendships that don't seem like they'll stick but eventually do. Alcohol, romance, night buses, tears, heartbreak, homesickness, vomit, regret, glamorous settings for dinner, dingy dance-floors afterwards. The doors clicking on and off in the back seat of the black cab. Wine bottles clinking in a tote bag. Beer cans sweating in the evening sun. A feeling, against logic, that youth might yet be endless. A nightclub stamp that will not wash off the wrist. Men pissing in giant plastic troughs on the street, put there by the council. A party in an elegantly kitted-out Hackney Wick warehouse where I know almost nobody. A New Year's Eve when at midnight, we duck into the Spanish neighbours' loft and get lost in their strings of hundreds and hundreds of fairy lights. A Christmas party at Rebecca and Sam's with jugs of negroni and several metres of homemade sausage rolls. A kebab at E. Mono in Kentish

Town on the way home, chilli sauce on my chin. A dinner at Noble Rot where Lucy accidentally set the paper menu on fire. A party in the beautiful Bloomsbury home Rachel is house-sitting, where I make the mistake of drinking the Czech moonshine. A karaoke night where Karl and I, wildly out of character, sing 'Fairytale of New York' in front of a room full of strangers, and unexpectedly bring one woman to tears. A premature nostalgia for this very moment. One Saturday in December, I criss-cross the city to attend four different parties. I go from Manor House to Tottenham Hale, then onwards to Marble Arch and finally south, on a crawling bus, to Camberwell. All of these things that come back to mind on seeing the dress discarded at the end of the bed, in the cold light of the following day.

Aoife and I get through a few more beers, a couple of packets of crisps. When the pub rings the bell for last orders, we stand to leave. Beside us the two fabulous women do the same, and while we are putting on our coats, I gesture to Aoife. I tell her that I'd been struck by their glamour earlier, that I hadn't been able to stop watching them while I waited for her arrival. She turns, subtly, to check them out.

'Ana,' she says, a little amused. 'They're just two pretty girls wearing nice clothes.'

We part with a hug at the bus stop. I hop on to the 4 and sit upstairs. Pretty girls, nice clothes. Now I am reminded of a night some time ago, sitting in the bar at St John.

I am with Rebecca, watching her eat a plate of devilled kidneys when the celebrity arrives. The celebrity is tall and dynamic and beautiful – you'd turn to watch her entering a room even if she wasn't famous. She is wearing an elegant 1940s kind of coat, inky black with a prim little collar, and very expensive shoes, and she is with a gaggle of well-dressed men who look like creative directors for fashion brands that just got financial backing. I am tired, and have been tired, of London recently – wary that the things I once found fascinating about this city are starting to feel draining instead. The celebrity's arrival is a riposte to all of that. Look, it seems to say, here, you live cheek by jowl, you scrimp and save to pay for evenings like these, but you also live beside intense glamour. Later, when the celebrity slips outside for a cigarette, we see she has shed her coat to reveal a gorgeous concoction of black tulle, like something we would only have seen on tiny models at fashion week. Not here in the wild, eating dinner next to us!

'She is so glamorous,' Rebecca whispers with great excitement, as if her presence has affirmed our own excellent taste somehow. As if it maybe even makes the food we eat taste better.

There are things that happen here only when the sun goes down. For one thing, the dial of London's sophistication is more easily turned up. Concoctions of black tulle and very expensive shoes worn by statuesque women seem more fitting after dark. The night-time, when we commit to it, is intoxicating. The smallest and most incidental thing – getting into a black cab or buying a packet of cigarettes in a corner shop – can feel different when I am dressed for the night. My clothes make more sense, too, feeling less like costume and more like a prescribed uniform of glamour: black velvet or brown suede, a rash of sequins or a panel of ruched silk. Things I saved up for, or hunted down online, or splurged on when I couldn't afford to. They are more sumptuous in these hours, and this makes me feel worthier, in a way. Like maybe I deserve to be here more when it's dark and I'm dressed up.

For a few hours, Rebecca and I chat as we eat and drink well, with a feeling almost as though we are celebrating something. In a way maybe we are. The arrival of the celebrity gave the night an extra patina of sorts – a story to recount after the fact – but maybe we don't need it. Outside, the street is misty with the first fog of the season. Cooler weather is on its way. I think of the gloom of foggy winter mornings here, my workaday woollen coat growing damp on the walk to the Tube. My beautiful clothes packed away at the back of the wardrobe, awaiting their next outing. Even the weather is more intriguing in the evening. When at last we leave the restaurant, there is mist hanging in the air, making the streetlights near Smithfield Market look eerie and haloed, like medieval portraits of saints.

YASHANA MALHOTRA

Fashion designer, big-dress aficionado

Where did you grow up?

I grew up in India. I moved to the UK when I was seven, to Yorkshire, where I grew up. I moved to London for uni, and it's been about five years now that I've been here. But my family lives in Yorkshire, and the rest of them are in India and everywhere else.

So home is Yorkshire, or India?

I would say home is London. Obviously, where the family is, that's also home. But this is a different kind of home, because I feel most myself here.

Would you say that living in London has changed you?

I think you adapt to the speed of it. Everything is so fast. I remember the first day I came here from Yorkshire with my little suitcase. I was at King's Cross station, and I just sat there for a moment. All these people passed me so fast, and I was so intimidated.

You're currently finishing your studies at Central Saint Martins, but I first saw you on Instagram, where you'd posted images of yourself in these huge elaborate dresses that you'd made, wearing them in ordinary situations, on the Tube, or walking down a street in Shoreditch. I imagine that you turn a lot of heads when you go out in them.

When I make the dresses, I'm doing it for me, not anybody else. But it's nice that I can go outside, walk around in them and people will actually get to see them.

When you're making a dress, do you think about how they look in the city? Like, 'OK, I need to see how this works on the street before I know if it works as a dress.'

I mean, I don't think I consider it that much, but in the back of my mind it must be there. Because some dresses do really well – most of them get a reaction, but if one gets a lot of reaction, you get an idea of what people like about a dress, you know? It's like doing a survey every time you walk outside.

I was thinking about this the other day, why so many people look at the dresses when I wear them. I guess it's because other people don't dress like that. It's literally that simple. It's not because they're great, or they're this or that. It's just because you don't see people in these kind of clothes on the street.

What is it that you like about wearing a big dress?

They're just comfortable, you know. They're not *princess* dresses, but they're just very excessive and when do we get to be excessive? Especially during lockdown, when people aren't even stepping out of the house, and there's me walking down the street in these dresses that are just massive. I just think it's fun to be honest. I don't see anything wrong with it.

You mentioned the pleasure of wearing it - I think it's something we forget a lot about clothes. And I'm sure that sometimes people see you and might feel motivated to wear something pleasurable of their own. Maybe they think something like, 'Oh, she's wearing a big dress and she loves it, maybe I could wear something that I really love.'

It's amazing if I can inspire even one person to step outside their comfort zone. Even if it's little kids. Yesterday I was wearing this pink dress with my pink Crocs. And there was this tiny girl with her mum, and her little scooter. She was really excited looking at me, and her mum was like, 'She loves your dress!' And the girl was like, 'No, I love the shoes!'

Are there any practical considerations when you get dressed? If you get on the Tube and it's packed, are you thinking, 'Oh my god, my dress is too big for this'?

No, absolutely not. I don't care about that at all. Of course it's hilarious, trying to get into some Tube carriage when it's packed and you're in this huge gown. But it's fine. The worst that people can do is say, 'This is ridiculous.' And I know! I think it's important to take up space, whether it's on a Tube, or in a classroom, or outside.

Is that something you always thought, or has it come from studying and living here?

I think probably from living here. And especially the past year. It was quite formative in terms of the pieces I wear now. I was making a dress yesterday and I was like, this is so excessive. It's a pink taffeta one. The sleeves are huge – three metres of fabric, just in the sleeves. It is excessive. But I'm so comfortable in them.

When you're making a dress, do you ever think, while making it, god, this will look great on the Tube, or in a certain part of London?

Not as much. To be honest the backgrounds of my photos would be much more different if it didn't come down to where I can find something to rest my phone on. If there's no ledge, I can't do that. So if I see some background or if I'm crossing the street or something I'm like, 'This looks great! But obviously there's nothing for me to rest my phone on to film it!'

I love doing it on the Tube. Just put your phone down on the seat, sit down, get up, it's done. If I see a spot with a ledge, I just put my phone there. The dresses don't blend perfectly into the background, but there's some connection to it I think, even if the colours are opposite or not quite the same. The backgrounds bring the photos to life I think, equally as much as the dress. You know, I don't want a white background.

And we don't wear clothes on a runway or against photo paper. We wear them on the street.

Exactly. That's also why I take them outside, in those very real spaces, because it's saying: this is real life. I haven't dressed up just to take this picture before getting changed or being any different. The other day I was sitting having a fag near St Paul's and there were these girls, influencers I guess, they brought this suitcase with them. I was watching them and they take a photo, change into a different outfit from the suitcase, take another photo, then get changed and leave. They go home. That's so weird.

How do you feel in the dresses when you wear them at home in Yorkshire?

Not as great as in London. Sometimes with my friends in Yorkshire, they ask, 'Why are you wearing such a big dress? We're in the country, everyone knows us.' I'm like, 'Well, why would you care about that?' But they get more anxious about it than I do. No, to be fair, I wouldn't change the way I dress just because I'm in the country. People here are used to seeing people, and I think Londoners to an extent don't care: Do what you want, it's not my business. Country people however are a different story. But then again, I don't care, so that's fine. If you want to tell Janet from across the street that I'm wearing a big dress, that's fine.

My mum can be a bit like, 'Are you really going out like that?? Can you just wear joggers today?' I'm like, 'Mum, NO!' Why should I have to change how I am just because I'm in a different place? Of course, I do feel much more comfortable wearing them in London.

It's strange when you go home. It feels like it's difficult sometimes to bring your 'London self' with you.

London must be the best place for people to just be however they are. I can't imagine any other place being as open or diverse. It's not about being accepted for who you are. It's just about the British culture of not caring, multiplied by people being too busy in their own lives to care about you. All of these factors make it perfect to just do what you want, wear what you want, be what you want, you know? People just don't have the time to care. They'll see something and be like, [droll voice] *Great.* Or they'll be like, [unimpressed voice] *What the fuck.* Or people will see what you're wearing, and just not have a thought about it. You get all of that in one city.

8. At the Tate Modern

I groan when I see the queue for Christian Marclay's *The Clock*, winding down the staircase of the Blavatnik Building at the Tate Modern. It is a Sunday afternoon, and I feel, briefly, cheated: being forced to wait because the thing I want to do is the thing that everyone else here wants to do.

It is no real surprise that there is a queue. *The Clock* is popular among Londoners this autumn. I myself have waited years for the opportunity to see it: a 24-hour-long video that stitches together clips from thousands of films in which clocks and watches feature. The result is that Marclay's artwork functions as an actual timepiece, in that viewers are watching an endless succession of images of the time at that very moment as it marches relentlessly on, in clip after clip from across the history of cinema. I have been sneaking out from my office nearby on my lunch breaks, to snatch a twenty- or thirty-minute piece of *The Clock*. I slip into the dark gallery – no queues at that time of day – and sit alone in the dark and eat my lunch quietly.

Weekends, however, are a different story. The queue moves slowly, and so I pass the time by looking. A few metres ahead of me is a couple. They're older, and he's got unruly white hair and some Camper Oxfords and she's in a sculptural necklace like something Prue Leith would wear. I look further along the queue and see restless Italian teenagers with backpacks, one carrying a perfect red leaf from a plane tree that you could frame and keep as a relic of a London autumn. There are kissing couples, a girl who I can hear asking her Brutalism-tote-carrying boyfriend – at the top of the queue, after queuing here for at least thirty minutes! – 'What are we queueing for, anyway?' And there's a woman alone with her headphones, in Dr. Martens and high-waist denim and a shrunken Harrington jacket, looking at her phone, shuffling forward with the queue.

There are groups who've come straight from Dover Street Market, in Off-White t-shirts and tangerine socks, bearing carrier bags loaded with their designer purchases. Englishwomen with straight fringes and mustard cardigans and tote bags with slogans about reading. North London gay couples, the type who go to everything, every weekend, with silvering hair and a copy of Ben Lerner's *10:04* visible in a coat pocket. A pregnant woman and an excited child, who seems to know more about *The Clock* than the adults.

I mean, I could go on and on. The queue certainly does. These are the places you often avoid on weekends. It becomes part of your identity as a Londoner, to reject the tumult on your days off. To say that living in the city, something you have presumably elected to do, is too much for you. Too crowded. But there is something quite good about the crowd when you just give in to it. Here is the city: all of the people who go to the Tate Modern on a sunny Sunday afternoon to look at some art indoors, simply because that's what people in London do. All of the people who want to do the same thing as you. Here we are, waiting for time to pass so we can take our place in the dark and sit together in silence.

9. Walking

There seem to be more of them with every year that passes. Scattered across the city like a patchwork quilt of unusually pristine colour-coded spaces. They seem to be carved out of nothing: what was previously wasteland or some mark on the map that had been deemed unimportant is now organised neatly, branded in friendly colours and shapes on posters. They usually have new names, based on the history of the place where they stand, but often with an aspirational word thrown in – Reach, More, Plaza. When I enter one, I can't quite tell where I am, or why, and that's usually when I realise I've found one of London's privately owned public spaces.

They can feel, sometimes, like any other street or square in the city. Maybe cleaner and bedecked with more bunting than my own street. They might be municipal, but in a way that doesn't quite feel democratic, like the area around London

City Hall on the southern bank of the Thames, where there are restrictions against protest. Or they may be commercial spaces designed by the world's leading architects, beautiful open-air malls that bear no resemblance to the sprawling shopping centres of my youth. These places rarely have the funnelled chaos, the noises and bustle that I might find walking from Tottenham Court Road station through Soho's messy grid. They might be rigged with CCTV and even facial recognition technology; often they are patrolled by private security guards in hi-vis jackets who make me feel wary.

In London, for centuries there have been parts of the city that are not open to the public. These include places that today we'd stroll without a second thought – historic and upmarket neighbourhoods such as Portland Place by Regent's Park – as well as streets like Kensington Palace Gardens, where pedestrians are free to walk but must do so overlooked by heavily armed guards stationed outside embassies. The privately owned public spaces that interest me most, however, are not closed-off residential communities in leafy districts, but the ones that hide in plain sight, masquerading as the commons with profit in mind. These spaces are a filtered, purified version of the city, more family-friendly and more corporate than whatever I expected from London when I first arrived.

My decision to come to the city rested on an admissions interview in an upstairs room on Charing Cross Road. I came alone for the day, flying in early in the morning and making my way from Gatwick Airport to Soho with my notebook and my folder of clippings proudly stashed in my tote bag. At the entrance to the old Central Saint Martins building, I moved past students who were smoking on the steps, crowding the pavement in black, with combat boots, torn trousers, dyed hair, coloured tulle, battered Louis Vuitton handbags. They were loud, sharing jokes and talking about class and where they'd go out that night, and I dawdled among them for a few seconds as I entered the building, thinking how close I was to being part of this kind of new city noise.

I walked up a flight of stairs and along a corridor lined with classroom doors. Everywhere there was a gentle disorder, the kind that comes from so many young and energetic people in close quarters. Maybe I was wide-eyed about it, but I thought I could feel the energy in the air: ideas, creativity, sure, but also secrets and stories, gossip, friendships and rivalries and all the stuff of private lives. It was a fabled building that had been occupied by many of the country's most brilliant artists and designers in recent history. This building was not just where they learned their craft. It was also where they lived their lives for a little while. It was more than alluring to think that I could occupy it, too. I felt giddy with it by the time I entered my admissions interview.

The interview was brief, testing. I babbled on confidently about my experience, my desires for my career, my plans for the summer after graduating. The two lecturers interviewing me asked me to wait outside for ten minutes after it ended, and then brought me back in to tell me I'd been accepted. My heart pounded as I left the building and wound my way back down to the street through design studios and classrooms where I saw students wrestling with sculptures and dresses and canvases. All of it would be mine, I thought to myself. I spent the rest of the day wandering around the city, imagining the life I would be able to have here in mere months now – the vast unruliness of what now awaited me.

Six months later, I moved to London to begin my masters. In that time, the university had shuttered the rattling old building on Charing Cross Road and moved to a pristine converted warehouse just north of King's Cross station. The building, with its high open atrium, was impressive to look at. But it was strange and slightly aloof to study in, and the location had none of the in-the-thick-of-it charm of Soho. This was new London, pre-2012-Olympics London. There was nothing around the school except for building sites and goods vehicles. Every morning that first winter I walked up a long pedestrian road that was lined with construction hoardings and cranes. Someday it would be packed with offices and shops, but for now it was just a nameless sloping road connecting the Tube station to the new building, and the wind seemed to tunnel right through me no matter which direction I walked.

Ten years on, I come back to the area on a rare day off. In the time since I studied there, the space around the university has bloomed like a hothouse garden. First a restaurant, then an airy and bright supermarket, and now an entire shopping mall built into a Victorian storage yard for coal that once arrived by train at the station nearby.

What is now known as Coal Drops Yard is possibly the most pleasant privately owned public space I know of in London. Much work has gone into making it feel like an *authentic* experience in some way, and I'm aware immediately that it is geared towards people in the same demographic as me, in terms of how we spend our time and our money: university-educated with a certain amount of disposable income in the pocket, fond of cultural activities and eager to keep up with the trends. It would be more surprising if it didn't register as *pleasant* for me on some level. Pleasant boutiques, pleasant outposts of favourite Soho restaurants, set into the old walls of the yard. It even has pleasant little laneways to explore, like a real neighbourhood in a foreign city I might visit on a weekend away. A little fake piazza with red metal tables and chairs, where I can rest when my feet grow weary from all the browsing in the pleasant shops.

So I try to enjoy it. Yet for all its pleasantness, it still rings false. I step into a clothing boutique. I haven't been shopping recently. Inside, in the gleaming clean space with its kind mirrors and optimal lighting, I gather an armful of clothes and head to the fitting room. I try on some new things for the first time in a while – a pair of ecru-coloured flares with a very high waist, a polyester polka-dot dress with a daring slit on one side. I don't need new clothes and yet almost without my noticing, I glide to the cash register and pay for a new t-shirt. I feel a brief, intense hit of dopamine as I head back outside. I don't need this t-shirt. I can't justify spending money on an unnecessary t-shirt at this moment. But I feel compelled to buy it, my movements determined for me like a pinball dropped into a machine.

Then I walk to the piazza and sit down at a bright red metal table and chair in the sun, and I open my notebook to take notes. Beside me, three Central Saint Martins students chat in Cantonese between classes. Nearby, children play minigolf on a set painted in Memphis-like colours, scattered around the piazza. Couples stop and queue for tables outside restaurants. All of this, I notice, takes place under the watchful gaze of two security guards in hi-vis vests that may or may not be stab-proof, but certainly are designed to look stab-proof.

I am used to the presence of such men when I am in public in London. When I first moved here, I was unnerved by the sight of police at St Pancras train station casually wielding their submachine guns. During the following years, there were terror attacks in London, Manchester, Paris – places familiar to me – which seemed to necessitate the presence of armed police, if not in my own mind then at least in the mind of the public. Not all police were armed, not everywhere, but enough of them that if something terrible did happen, that somewhere, there would be a hero with a gun to stop the villain, apparently. This was how the narrative went, and so their presence was meant to soothe and allow city dwellers to move freely around the city, about their business. This was the real victory against the terrorists, of course, that we would not live in fear, that terrorism would not stop us from living our lives.

But I don't know. The sight of deadly weapons wielded by anyone has never made me feel safe in the city. In places like this piazza, the security guards obviously do not wield heavy-duty firearms. The guards stationed around the place are not bothered with the likes of me. They look bored, and I look like I might spend money here, evidenced especially by the carrier bag at my feet. Certainly, I'm not giving any indication that I might cause them hassle. But this could change at a moment's notice. I imagine myself standing up from the red metal chair and doing something odd – lying down on the ground, for instance, or screaming for no reason. Or what if, on some occasion, I had reason to protest here? I imagine that the security might ask me to stop what I'm doing in that case. In fact, they would probably have the ability to remove me, if they wanted to, since spaces of this kind can enforce their own regulations, distinct from the rights citizens might have in truly public spaces.

And when they are unobtrusive like this, I do still notice them. I feel different when I am in their presence. As they watch me, I subconsciously watch myself, too, in a way I don't when I walk down a street without them. As a result, I find

I can't watch the world around me with as much ease. Here in Coal Drops Yard, that doesn't matter so much, because people like me are only here for the pleasure of consumption, spending money and precious free time on organised, for-profit leisure.

My unease in privately owned public spaces is not so much that the surveillance is visible, or that I don't feel free to lie down on the ground. These things play a role, of course. But the problem is what these spaces lack. They lack room for secrets, for chaos, for the vibes that accumulate over years and generations like they did in the old art college building on Charing Cross Road. Over the centuries, many writers have talked about their cities as palimpsest, endlessly made and remade with the histories of the people who lived and left their mark there. It is in part what attracts many people to these cities: the ability to write your own life into the life of the city's, even in some small way. But here in Coal Drops Yard, every inch is cleaned up and readied for the generation of profit. Even the art college seems to provide a layer of creative cultural cachet for the retail development. In reality, artists are priced out of cities like London, especially during regenerations like this one. Central Saint Martins attracts students from all over the world who come to London to study because of its rich heritage, its international outlook. Many of them – I know from the students I studied with – will rack up debt to live in dodgy accommodation somewhere far from the college. But for a few years, their lives – socially, intellectually, creatively, romantically – might revolve around the big brick building in King's Cross. Their art is in the windows, giving shoppers at Coal Drops Yard something to look at on their way to Waitrose. Then, when they graduate, many of them will be forced to leave when they can't afford the prohibitively expensive visas.

In her book *The Gentrification of the Mind*, the writer and activist Sarah Schulman examines the impact that gentrification and the AIDS crisis had on New York's avant-garde queer artists in the 1980s and 1990s. AIDS devastated this community and, in its wake, gentrification served to hollow out the physical spaces these artists had previously occupied. The effect of gentrification on artists is not just a means of pricing them out, she writes. It is also that:

> They are faced with conformity of aesthetics and values in their neighborhoods. Conventional bourgeois behavior becomes a requirement for surviving socially, developing professionally, and earning a living. By necessity, their goals are altered. Reimagining the world becomes far more difficult, and reflecting back what power brokers and institutional administrators think about themselves feels essential to survival . . . There seems to be no other game in town.

Maybe it's that I have been sold a lie. Maybe I was told, for a long time, that there were many different games in town – that was part of the town's appeal. But when I walk through these strange, clean urban spaces, I find that there is no room here for so much of what had attracted me to city life in the first place.

* * *

In all the years I've lived here I have never taken one of the commuter boats that trip along the Thames. On a sunny bank holiday afternoon, I board near Westminster, tagging on with my debit card as though I were hopping on to the 390 bus. The boat is easily the most pleasant form of public transport I've stepped foot on in London. A breeze, a nice view. There is even a bar. I take a seat at the open rear of the boat and watch the London Eye and the Houses of Parliament ebb away as we head west along the water. The boat is branded with the insignia of a ride-sharing app that I deleted from my phone a few years ago, for what I think were vaguely ethical complaints. But that doesn't take from the enjoyment I feel on board: wherever I am, anywhere on earth, I am content when I am being safely taken across water.

The boat pulls up near Battersea Park, and I disembark to find myself in a curving privately owned public space that runs along the river. In the shadow of the former Battersea Power Station, there are brightly coloured posters and flags, anonymous chain restaurants and picnic benches watched over by more bored security guards. There are signs that explain that these benches are 'Batter-seats' and are only for paying customers from the nearby restaurants. You can't sit and eat your own picnic here overlooking the river; in fact, if you brought a picnic, it would be best to keep on walking until you reach the public park. This landing is not a very comfortable or pleasant place, and the only reason I can think of for this is the imposition of money on the casual, easy city roaming I had been doing before I disembarked the boat. The prioritisation of paying customers over city walkers feels like a stop sign being held up to my face by an overzealous traffic warden. I pass quickly through this place, stopping only to use their well-appointed portacabin toilets, and then I cross Chelsea Bridge to the north side of the Thames Embankment.

The stretch of Chelsea Embankment from Millbank as far as the World's End estate is one of my favourite arcs of the city to walk: a busy road, a tree-lined quiet footpath, a calming view of the river on one side and on the other, some of London's finest historic homes. What more could you want? There is an awful lot of clutter built up against the river in this city; a lot of shoddy luxury apartments constructed more as tax shelters and investments rather than as homes. When my boat passed the section of river between Vauxhall and Nine Elms I glanced at the apartments that litter the riverside there. I thought *mistake, mistake* over and over in my head. But here on the north side of the river, with the plane trees and the remnants of the sixteenth-century home of

St Thomas More, there is a greater sense of what this place was like long before I was born.

It was not always possible to stroll along the riverbank here. First there had to be an embankment to walk on. Before there was an embankment, there was acre after acre of swampy marshland instead. Waste was emptied directly into the Thames as early as the 1300s, and for a long time, nobody would want to come too close to the water, because of the sewage and the smell. As the city grew more sprawling and industrialised, sewers and factory outfalls all over the city led to the river, where human waste and industrial effluent flowed directly into the water. In warm weather, this created a noxious smell that made Londoners sick. By 1858, the smell was so bad it had a name – the Great Stink – and a disgusting illustrated persona that cropped up in periodicals like *Punch* – Father Thames, a muddy Poseidon, who in one cartoon is shown 'introducing his children (Diphtheria, Scrofula and Cholera) to the fair city of London'. The smell was so bad that summer that politicians noticed it coming in through the windows of the Houses of Parliament at Westminster, not far from where I walk now. The curtains were doused in lime chloride to absorb some of the smell, and cabinet ministers conducted meetings with handkerchiefs over their noses to avoid breathing it in.

In the wake of the Great Stink the construction of the Thames Embankment finally went ahead, in 1862, after decades of failed attempts. This involved narrowing the channel of the river, lining its new path with granite brought by barge from Lamorna Cove in Cornwall. The granite was much anticipated by many in the city. *The Times* wrote of looking forward to seeing 'thirty-four acres of slime' replaced with a 'wall of solid masonry', 'a handsome parapet and bold granite mouldings'. The main motivation behind the project of embanking the Thames was the creation of a sewage system, the work of the visionary civil engineer Joseph Bazalgette. It was hoped that this would end the recurrent cholera epidemics that had afflicted London's neighbourhoods earlier in the 1800s, and sort out the smell once and for all. (Even today, though, sewage is still dumped directly into the river at least once a week. I learn this from a hoarding covering some works for the so-called super sewer near Chelsea Bridge. The signage from Thames Water, the company behind the works, reminds me that it's 'your river', and I smile to myself, because it is.) The sewer system did bring with it some new problems, too. Methane gas began building up underground, occasionally exploding at pavement level. But this elicited another visionary idea: in the 1890s, the inventor Joseph Webb patented the Sewer Gas Extractor and Destructor, a lamp which could ventilate the methane gas while also lighting up the street itself by using the gas as fuel. These lamps were installed all over the country, particularly in hilly urban areas where such gases built up. London's only surviving example can be found tucked behind the Savoy hotel on Carting Lane, though today it runs on gas from the mains and not the sewer.

But the embanking project also served to put order on a part of the city that was wilder, more unruly, than the streets and churches and buildings that comprised the rest of London. Nature itself could be lined elegantly in granite, it turned out.

As I walk along the Chelsea Embankment, I realise how strange it is to think of this most natural element of the city as almost man-made in its form. The river feels so timeless, so ancient, that it is odd to think of it looking so utterly different only 150 years ago. It is also difficult to conceive of the vision required for a project like this – the imagination and will to civilise such a large part of the landscape, to bring it into line with the cultivated fabric of the city itself. Embanking the Thames reclaimed around twenty-two acres of land and changed the lives and health of almost everyone who lived in the city. Now when we hear about visionary projects in London, the words usually refer to another privately owned public space, or a new pointless skyscraper that will achieve nothing and remain off-limits to most Londoners. The act of sanitising the city – something that had been integral to making London a better and cleaner place to live in – is now part of a project that is more concerned with making it easier to extract profit from the city and those who live and work here.

On the embankment I smell blossom from the Chelsea Physic Garden, and traffic fumes. The hoarding that informs me about the super sewer and the weekly flows of sewage into 'your river' astounds me – not the fact of the pollution, but the fact that I think so little about my river, my sewage. It's so easy to forget about it here. The last time I came so close to it was in 2018. That spring, the Museum of London had opened *Fatberg!*, an exhibition centred on a chunk of a so-called fatberg excavated from the sewers below Whitechapel. A fatberg is a solid mass of congealed grease, wet wipes, nappies and condoms that builds up in a sewer, and such fatbergs block sewers in cities all over the world. They're dangerous and hazardous, hard work for sewage workers to deal with. The Whitechapel fatberg, discovered in 2017 and weighing in at over 130 tonnes, took two months for Thames Water workers to destroy. The Museum had decided to acquire a slice of it for their display, and so, on its opening weekend, I rode the bus to the City of London and queued up to see the fatberg, a line of curious Londoners ahead of me. We waited patiently for our turn to look at the foot-long lump of coagulated oil, rubbish and human waste. When I got to peer into the glass cabinet, I saw flies that had hatched from maggots inside it. A woman behind me retched quietly into her hand. I took a blurry photo of the fatberg, which was itself disintegrating slowly before my eyes. Later on, I realised that my phone's AI system had categorised it as a photo of cake.

The exhibition was not just a chance to come face to face with my own waste for once. It also had a moral to it. The curators made clear that as citizens of this metropolis with its Victorian sewers, we should not flush nappies or condoms down the toilet, and we shouldn't pour our oil down the sink, either. I nodded, reading this, and looked at the next exhibit: a protective suit of clothing worn by the people who excavated the fatberg. I imagined the weary Thames Water worker removing her suit at the end of the shift, showering thoroughly before going home to regale the family with tales of the day's work down in the dark sewer. There was an emotional narrative that ran all through the *Fatberg!* exhibition, a familiar, age-old story: man's battle against a kind of fairy-tale monster, the ogre or dragon that must be defeated to save the townspeople. But the exhibition also made clear that fatbergs – disgusting things – are the unavoidable by-products of so many people living in one place. That it is right that we should come face to face with them, once in a while, even if only behind glass at a museum.

We lose so much when swaths of the city are sanitised. Not just a chance to be confronted with the worst parts of ourselves, but the choice to be free, to be filthy if we want to be. This is how we learn how to be citizens of the city, people who know how to live here happily. This learning can't happen in bedrooms or cramped communal kitchens in flat-shares. It happens in public, and we do it incidentally, through looking, through paying attention to the world around us. It is harder to do this under surveillance or restrictions, or in a space that is designed to generate profit from those who pass through it. Shared spaces – streets and sewers and parks and plazas which belong to all who use them – are the literal common ground that can hold a city together. It's here that there is room for so much to accumulate over centuries. Waste, yes, but also the histories and secrets of those who pass through them. This is what makes the city so vital, so real and so enduringly attractive to newcomers. They never cease to come here, allured by some idea of the rough magic of London life. They, and I, pass through it like the Thames itself, leaving bits of ourselves behind as we go.

10. Walking (passeggiata)

It is 6 p.m. on a warm night, and everyone in the Sicilian city of Palermo is out; the street is thronged with people. Teenagers with ironed hair peel off from their parents to congregate by the ice cream shop. Flashy men in beautiful suits and sunglasses steer their partners through the melee, faces tilted upwards. Elderly couples in their finest – a man in a brown linen suit and a wonderful blue bow tie, a woman with bright red lipstick and an elegantly carved cane. Over and over, people greet each other with a surprise that isn't really a surprise, like bumping into a co-worker in the office kitchen. Everyone else is here, so why wouldn't you be, too?

'Passeggiata' is the Italian word for the leisurely, pleasurable stroll taken in the golden light of the evening. It is a social activity. This is not a stroll taken for health or exercise so much as an opportunity to see your friends, and to be seen by all and sundry. Interactions that might usually take place in private homes, or at least in semi-private spaces such as restaurants or bars, are part of the public realm here. If you find yourself on a busy Italian street just before dinnertime, especially on a Sunday evening, you'll notice that people dress up for passeggiata. They make the most of the flattering evening light in the clothes they want to show off. If you are a tourist who ends up in the melee on her way to grab an evening beer in her shorts and sandals, skin sticky with old sunscreen, well, you're going to feel a little underdressed.

In a small Italian town or an individual neighbourhood, the passeggiata is a very clear way to foster belonging among a community: everyone seems to come out of their homes at the same time of day and they walk together, greeting, chatting or just looking at each other. But in a big city without outlets for community, it is easy to feel like you don't belong. This is why so-called third places are so important. A third place is a neutral space outside the home where people can relax, interact and gather together. It's not your workplace, which is your second place. The term was coined by the American sociologist Ray Oldenburg in his book *The Great Good Place*, and it was Oldenburg's belief that the presence of third places is necessary for a democracy that works and a society that is fair and nourishing for those living within it.

In normal times, a city like London doesn't have a direct equivalent of the Italian passeggiata, but it does have a hundred different ways for a citizen to go out and see people.

In a city under lockdown, however, there is only the park. Oldenburg says that one important function of the third place is the potential for the informal, unplanned run-in, the sight of a familiar face, without the chain of texts and emails and phone calls that tends to precipitate it. The bar, the coffee shop, the barber or the gym or the nail salon: they facilitate what Oldenburg calls 'informal public life'. This is something I keenly feel the absence of during lockdown. When the city is closed, it's the park that becomes the load-bearing location for city dwellers: a plaza, a theatre, a public place that can be shared among the people.

On a grey January weekday morning, I dress myself in layers and scarves and cross-body bags until I feel like a sentient coat stand, a totem pole draped in fabric. Then I grab my keys and head for the park. At the moment these daily walks are my only time outside the house, and the park's muddy paths are used only by lone walkers. The people who came prepared in wellington boots and anoraks are the ones who seem to enjoy it most. I pass a small, grey-haired woman in a grey walking jacket and Nordic poles – mustard tights, mustard gloves, mustard hat. Elsewhere, a smart quilted coat. A woman with a shock of white-blonde curls, shouting at a similarly coloured labradoodle. Perhaps it's not that we've shed vanity, but that vanity has taken on new forms. I see the walkers in the park like flags of errant nations, the way yachts must display theirs in harbour. Even in clothes I don't think about, don't invest anything emotional into, I am aware that I'm still dressing myself – my *self*. I am ascertaining the outlines of my selfhood at a time when those outlines are blurred through lack of normal routine and an absence of informal public life and the benefits it brings.

Most days, I don't know how I am feeling until I go outside. Then I can gauge my mood on the basis of how I respond to the sight of a dog in a fluorescent jacket that reads NERVOUS, or a man my father's age sitting alone on a bench, scarf tucked carefully into his collar, hands folded in his lap. Now we are here, I think. I am here, seeing others and being seen by them, while we all do the same thing. It creates a kind of fellow feeling that I think is necessary for happiness, and for connection, especially in a city. I tread carefully through the mud, and head back to the flat for another afternoon of work.

* * *

In the United Kingdom, the public park was first conceived as a solution to a problem. The problem, as it arose during the nineteenth century, was how to occupy the free time of the newly created urban working classes. Without space for morally good recreation it was feared that the new class of working men would use their leisure time in destructive ways – drinking, worst of all. Give the people a park, and they would have somewhere to bring their families. They would get dressed up to amble around in public. In this way, urban green spaces came to represent a moral good, and something for everyone, not just the wealthy elite. New public parks were created, or in some cases converted from private use, with this in mind: for the benefit of the populace, for the purposes of leisure.

In early lockdown, the local park became a space fraught with a kind of moral panic. This is unsurprising, considering the vast weight that public parks had to bear as one of the only places where people could legally go. Guidelines in this country said that outdoor exercise was permitted, and that parks were to be left open, though at first, driving to the park was not allowed. Transport was to be done by foot or by bicycle, meaning parks were accessible mostly for those who were lucky enough to live close by them. Near my flat, the paths were alive with anxiety. Walkers kept a performative two-metre distance from each other, as per the guidelines, and cohabiting couples were criticised for holding hands. Could they not do that at home?

As the weather warmed in April, images of sunbathers landed on front pages and on social media. The newspapers embarked on a new programme of lockdown shaming. How dare these selfish people lie in the sunshine? Don't they know there is a pandemic on?

Later on, we learned that lying on the grass at a distance from other people presents a viral risk so low as to be negligible.

But at the time the very idea of leaving the four walls of one's home was said to be intensely dangerous, both personally and for the wider community. Police around the country used drones to spot walkers in the hills. Parks released statements warning the public against breaking the rules and in some cases, against using the parks at all, lest the staff feel forced to close due to overcrowding. This did briefly happen in Victoria Park in Hackney and Brockwell Park in south London, parks with fences and gates that could be locked. I felt for my friends who lived in cramped flats near these parks, with no outside space and little inside space of their own.

During lockdown I walk alone. I live in a tiny one-bedroom flat without a garden, thirty-two square metres for Karl, our cat and me. The park becomes the only escape available, the one window of time I can be away from my home, and among other people.

Even when the parks in the other corners of the city are locked, mine is open. My local park cannot be locked. It has no gates: just grassy verges that meet the road without fanfare. Hampstead Heath is a 790-acre open space already widely mythologised in books and cinema. It is known for cruising, wild swimming and the occasional celebrity sighting. Among many, it is a by-word for a kind of well-heeled denizen of London, the kind of person who lives in one of the multi-million-pound mansions that line its verges. But many other different kinds of people walk on the Heath. I know this because I am one of them, and on my walks, I have seen others of them.

On these daily walks I try to imagine what it would have been like to be a Victorian Londoner at the time of the opening of the public parks. The first day, in 1835, that the gates of the Regent's Park were opened to the public. To be a woman out in the public realm with my family, seeing the neighbours, the men my husband or father worked with, and their families. I know better than to romanticise the past, but nevertheless I also know the excitement, the pleasures of time spent outside among other people, all of us purposeless and enjoying ourselves. That's the thread that connects me to the walkers of past iterations of this city, whether the city is open or locked down.

On lockdown weekends, Hampstead Heath's paths are thick with people. Wealthy families park Land Rovers nearby and clog the pavement with children and scooters. Dog-walkers in weather-worn anoraks and wellington boots frown at the other walkers. Despite the fact that daily exercise is one of the only reasons to be out of the home, joggers cause particular consternation; on several occasions I run past parents who shield their children from me and adults who press their faces towards the wall until I'm gone, as though I am a contagious travelling blob of virus, splattering coronavirus with every step.

Yet despite the risks, and despite how frustrating walking in a particularly crowded park can be, parks became a venue for social theatre during London's lockdown. They become, essentially, a place for passeggiata. The overriding early messaging concentrating on 'staying home' created a hunger in many for doing the very opposite. This included people with gardens, who still used the parks during the lockdown. The power of moral invective that made sunbathing worthy of scorn didn't extend as far as telling the wealthiest in the city to leave parks for those of us without gardens of our own. Everyone, apparently, can share the desire to get out of the house. Climbing a steep path to the top of Parliament Hill on another grey Tuesday afternoon, I fixate on this desire. What is it really expressing? I want to see people, and potentially, be seen by them, too. I want to feel like a part of a teeming mass, even just for an hour, in a way that is difficult when a potentially deadly virus is spreading rapidly through the population. So I go to the park to do a form of passeggiata of my own.

In the summer I looked for opportunities to wear the dresses I would've otherwise worn to restaurants or on holidays; in colder months, I eschew any idea of my own image. The weather turns, and we walkers stop dressing up so much. We go inside ourselves, even as we take ourselves outside. I tend to wear the same thing on my long walks on the Heath: a battered pair of mud-encrusted Nike Flyknit sneakers, a jumper knitted for me by my mother-in-law if the weather requires, one of three pairs of cotton canvas trousers I bought from Toast a couple of years ago. As the winter approaches in earnest, I don thermals, a woollen coat and hat. My vanity falls away with the dipping temperature.

* * *

By the middle of winter, there are more deaths from coronavirus every day than ever before. There is a new variant of the virus, and it seems to be spreading so quickly that we can no longer apply the previous rules of risk and logic that worked during the first year. There is talk of masks outside, or a ban on running.

The temperature drops and even the concrete paths in the park become sodden with mud. Blanket coats prevail, North Face puffers, actual hiking boots. I buy a cross-body pouch that fits my water bottle. It is the season of ruining footwear in the name of activity. Even courting frostbitten toes is better than another weekend afternoon on the couch with Netflix for company.

In early autumn, I am walking on the Heath when a man calls after me as I pass him on the winding path. It is the first time another walker has spoken to me in months, and I can feel myself flinch.

'Sorry,' he says. 'I'm only saying this because I love and respect footwear. The path you're taking, that way – it's really muddy.'

I look down at my battered Nike Flyknits. I chose these for today's walk because they are worn out and thin in places, destined shortly for the bin.

'I'm just letting you know. Because I'd hate to see you ruin your shoes.'

I nod, and thank him, and then I wait in place until he disappears from sight. Then I continue along the muddy path.

Slowly, the weather improves after a long, desolate winter, and I notice that weekend walkers start to add in their recent lockdown impulse purchases – a crisp new sweatshirt over the same old jeans, or a neon puffer jacket with muddy wellies. There is an intense optimism about this, and I love to see it. It is an acknowledgement, after so many long months of quiet, unobserved walking, that walking like this is a chance to be seen. And to be seen is to exist, in a way that is easily forgotten after so much time spent at home.

* * *

While I write this book, I suffer from a profound lack of physical and mental space. I use the word 'suffer' because it does feel like anguish. Our tiny flat has an open-plan style that means there are no doors between the living and bedrooms. During the pandemic Karl works long hours from home, taking many meetings on his laptop and leaving little space for a woman and her notebooks to clear her head. In regular times I would go to a coffee shop, a library, or even consider renting a desk space in another part of town. Instead I go for long walks on Hampstead Heath and around Crouch End and Belsize Park, stopping on street corners to tap notes into my phone. I press myself to the wall to let the other walkers pass me by.

Eventually, after many arguments with Karl, who can't do much as his office is closed and he must continue to earn money to pay the rent on our flat, a solution appears. One of my friends calls me. He has left his London flat to stay with his parents for a while, and he says I'm welcome to use it while he's gone. For a wonderful few weeks, my friend's empty living room becomes my third place. I walk, or take the train two stops, and sit very quietly on his sofa, with my laptop and my notebooks. I water his plants and eat my packed lunch at his kitchen table. I get more work done in a handful of afternoons than I have in months at home.

More than the ability to write, his flat provides me with something else I didn't realise I needed so badly during lockdown. For almost a year, the majority of my days have been loops of the same few streets, shops, sights, all in the same small radius around my house. Travelling to Farringdon offers me the chance to see new things, hear different noises. One afternoon I hear a familiar clomping and go to the window to see two police horses navigating the street below. Around the corner, passing through Hatton Garden on the way to the station, I notice that the district's renowned jewellery shops have emptied their windows during the lockdown. It is an uncanny sight.

And aside from the novelty of new sensory input, new interactions, my friend's flat gives me the chance to be myself in a different way. I am one person at home – my energy is different, my clothes are covered in cat hair – and another in the supermarket, or on my walks around the neighbourhood. Here I have a different kind of freedom to perform myself in public, on the journey to the flat, and then on arrival, to relax and focus. All these things seem to use different aspects of myself, in ways I couldn't access during the months I spent at my own home.

In the late afternoon, as the sky is getting dark, I pack up my work and leave the Farringdon flat. On the street outside, as I walk to the train station, I pass aimless wanderers and young men curiously positioned outside businesses that seem half-open, half-closed. A man in a wide-brimmed hat comes out of a shop drinking from a china teacup and he looks around the street; for a second we fall into step together as he ambles along. I watch men greet each other, one pulling up on his bicycle to clap a hand on the other's shoulder. They talk of business deals, diamond sales, when the shops might reopen. Everyone here seems to have a purpose, even the man with the teacup. Even me, walking from my own temporary workplace back to my home, my first place.

***

Now as I write I am still waiting for the city to wake up from its slumber. I've learned I cannot rouse it myself, tiptoeing around a sleeping giant. So I continue on my quiet walks, the ones that act as a salve for whatever I am bothered by on a given day. It always brings me some kind of relief. I can see other people. I can hear snippets of their conversation, and this jolts me from the monotony of my own thoughts. I can feel less isolated, more a part of the world. I am grateful for these interludes, as grateful as I have ever been. This too feels like a salve.

I am walking down Swain's Lane, thinking about the depths of isolation so many of us felt in the first days and weeks of the pandemic. In the early days of lockdown, before isolation became something we were good at, or at the very least, used to, people all over London gathered at their windows on Thursday evenings to clap in support of the NHS. At first I was sceptical, aware that frontline staff need personal protective equipment, better staffing levels, more pay, not applause.

But at 8 p.m. one Thursday I went to the windows. It is hard not to be near the windows, in such a small flat. In an instant I saw where everyone had been all this time: I saw the grid of lit-up yellow windows in the row of apartment blocks across the road. I saw old women in nightdresses on their balconies, wielding pots and wooden spoons. I saw a man I recognised from the park lean from his window with a trumpet at his lips; he blows a single glorious toot. I saw a child, barely more than an infant, held aloft in an apartment window, to be shown all the raucous commotion. Each window was like a little theatre stage, a little stamp-sized glimmer of the community we had been depriving ourselves of. The clap was bombastic, and I could hear rockets and bangers going off on the next street. At ground level, a Deliveroo cyclist freewheeled down the hill, looking upwards as he passed through the belly of the applause.

For a second, it seemed like it might not end, that we might not be able to stop ourselves. I was thinking of the dancing manias of Middle Ages Europe, where whole communities were driven by an unknown madness to dance until exhaustion. Days would go by and they'd dance until they collapsed in a heap on the ground. For a second, I was aware of how a collective madness like that might take hold – it felt so good to lean on my elbows and holler out my window, to look at the faces of my neighbours and feel them look at mine, too. Together we exerted ourselves, using body and voice to make an abstract thing feel real for just a little while.

NICOLA DINNEEN
Station supervisor, Canada Water station

What would make the difference between a good shift and a bad shift for you?

The service. It all depends on the service. If your service is OK and there's not too much happening [on the Transport for London network], then it's fine. But as soon as you've got those delays or suspensions, that's your bad shift.

What are your hours like?

I'm now part-time. I've worked at this station for twenty-three years, since before it opened. We did the set-up for it. Now I do Monday to Friday, 6.30 to 10.30 a.m., and I was mainly working on crowd control at the station in the mornings, when it used to be really, really busy.

And you're not working on crowd control at the moment.

Not now, because we don't have crowds. Pre-pandemic, our station, oh, we were as busy as Oxford Circus. It was packed downstairs on the platforms. People coming off the Overground, coming from West Croydon, Crystal Palace, Clapham – so many people take this route to get to Canary Wharf on the Jubilee Line. It cuts Zone 1 out, so your fare is cheaper. And then some come to travel westbound into the centre of London.

So what do you do on your shift now, if you're not doing crowd control?

You still have a lot of safety checks to do. Every room on the station gets checked over the course of a week. So you get your walk for the day – today I did Walk 1 where you check all the rooms on that walk for things like lights, equipment, the escalator machine chamber. Managing the staff, seeing where you need them deployed. There is less customer inter-action. We used to do things like helping people – people pass out on the train all the time, you need to be there to get them off the train. We don't have lots of things like that anymore. There's a lot less interaction with customers than there was. Now it's mainly when they need help on the gate-line [ticket barriers], help with directions, or they need help getting a ticket.

It's keeping things moving smoothly . . .

Yeah. For the people that are travelling, that are confident to travel. Be there and watch your platforms. It's not as hectic as it once was, and it can be a little bit boring.

Are you someone who likes the buzz?

Yeah, when I get in to work, I have my list of things to do and I'm going to work through and get it all done. I like to be busy.

How would you describe the commuters of Canada Water?

We have all different kinds of people. So, pre-pandemic, if you were going eastbound, it's more office-based workers, going to Canary Wharf. If you're going westbound, it's a mixture. You'll have people going on holiday [via airports], you'll have builders, retail workers. It's a big mixture. And obviously you have local people and then you have the interchange people.

Do you think there's a typical commuter within that?

If you came to my southbound platform in the morning, it's people getting off the westbound Jubilee – they're mainly builders. And they go to the southbound train. That was one of the things about the pandemic, construction workers were still travelling, and we were one of the stations that had a lot of construction workers. Eastbound, the office workers, is hardly anyone now. It's so funny, in the pandemic everyone stopped queueing [for the doors of the oncoming Jubilee train] because obviously you didn't need to. Now they've started to queue again.

Do you enjoy people-watching, observing all these people as they pass through the station?

Yeah. I worked in the control room for eighteen years, watching CCTV, watching out the window, keeping an eye on your staff, watching for anything that's not right. You're always watching. For me it's perfect – I could watch out the window all day.

Some people feel very energised by the presence of other people and some feel drained by it. How do you feel when you come off a shift?

If you've had a day where things have gone wrong and you literally haven't stopped – the service means you're giving alternative routes and you're constantly repeating the same thing constantly, and you'll try to address everyone and tell them and there's still someone going 'I didn't get that' – then that's a draining day. Sometimes people get upset if they can't get to work, and that's very draining. But by and large it's nice. It's nice when you help someone, or when they come back and say thank you, or pass on the message [through a colleague] to say, 'Oh, you let me use the loo when I was really not well, and I just wanted to say thanks for doing that.'

Have you had any memorable interactions with passengers?

God, it's too hard to think, because I've been here too long! You have nice customers who you like to see – there's an actor who comes through called Murray Melvin. He was in *Doctor Who* and he's a proper dapper guy, he's seventy-something. He's always so polite – he'll say good morning to you and ask if everything's alright. So you have customers like that who you remember.

I remember this lady who would come through – she worked for an airline, and she asked if she could use the loo and told me that she had leukaemia and was in treatment. So I let her use the loo. And she came back the next day and said thank you. And then you start to talk every time you see them – ask 'Where are you flying to today?' Things like that.

Have you ever seen anyone wearing anything that really caught your eye?

I always look at people's tote bags, I know that's really weird! But I love it when I'm on the platform and someone comes with an interesting tote. I used to write them down on my iPad, what they said, because some of them were so cool. Someone had a Ziggy Stardust quote and I was like, yay! Little sayings, little quotes, interesting-looking bags. Or band t-shirts – when you're into music, you see one and think, oh, I like that band!

Do you have to wear a uniform?

Yeah.

How do you feel about that?

Erm . . . [laughs] I prefer the old uniform. You do need to be able to be identified. When you're in a crowd, it makes it clear that you work in the station – you've got the uniform and you're there to help. You're knowledgeable and when you're a supervisor like I am, you're in control in situations that can arise. The uniform is part of all that. It's your identity for the four hours you're there.

And in a crowd, it's probably helpful for you to be able to find your colleagues as well.

Yeah, definitely. And if we have the hi-vis on, then you're really bright and you really stand out. We do need to be seen. If someone needs something, they need to be able to find you.

When you're going around the Tube in London, do you feel that different stations have different atmospheres?

Of course. If you go to Camden, you've got a younger crowd. Or Shoreditch – the minute you go to Shoreditch High Street everyone gets off, all the youngsters going out. Every one has slightly different kinds of people – Oxford Circus, you've got retail workers and the students and tourists.

Do you find yourself comparing things to your station?

I'm biased, but I love my station! I'm one of those people who still gets lost at Bank station.

Bank is very hard to navigate, I think. What have you learned about Londoners from your time on the Tube?

Everyone's in a rush to get to where they're going. That's just London. It doesn't relax. And that's the thing about the pandemic, it did make everyone slow down, restart. Slowly things are going back [to normal] and hopefully things'll be a bit different because everyone really does just want to get to where they're going – myself included. I think that you can't carry on like that forever. It really does take its toll; it can make you feel a bit wiped out and tired. I think the pandemic, although it's been bad, it has been good for people to slow down. They re-evaluate things, like how they travel around. I started cycling, and now I cycle to Bermondsey, rather than get the Tube.

Do you think Londoners have anything unique about them?

I don't know about other cities, but Londoners are not very good at change. If you have service disruption and you tell people, 'Look, I'm sorry, you'll have to go a different way' – I don't know what it is, but everything seems to go out the window in their mind. The minute there are any disruptions about, they can seem a bit lost, which I find surprising sometimes.

11. In Pond Square

Pond Square is the highest point in the borough of Camden
and was once home to two ponds that provided water for the
people of Highgate Village. In the late nineteenth century
the ponds were drained and the area made into an open
public space, owned by Camden itself. Today its lumpy trian-
gular shape is buttressed in each corner by a bank of over-
grown grass, ringed by low brick walls and a few benches. Tall
London plane trees are scattered unevenly around, forming a
canopy of shade in high summer.

Dogs are walked here. Children play, and friends sit
together on the grass or the brick wall. The benches provide
a place to relax for the drivers of the 271 bus, as it terminates
and turns around nearby, as well as for the retail workers
from the adjacent high street. Under one tree, a man clacks
away on a laptop. Across from him, two tennis players lounge

sweatily after their game at the courts in the park. Cyclists who have ascended Swain's Lane gather here to catch their breath before freewheeling down the hill to do it again. I don't know what compels them to do this. One summer I came here to see impromptu live music, and to take part in a series of local rallies for Black Lives Matter on weekend afternoons. In the lockdown winters, on Saturday mornings it was the closest thing the neighbourhood had to a piazza, with everyone out with their flasks of coffee and insulated jackets, circulating, and greeting one another.

The square is overlooked from each of its three-and-a-half sides by terraced houses built mostly in the eighteenth and nineteenth centuries. These houses are worth millions of pounds. My favourites are the five narrow ones on the north-western fringe, the slenderest of which is barely wide enough for a front door and a sash window. Their bricks sag with age and their front gardens are picturesque. Their front doors are painted in colours either cheerful or elegant – sunshine yellow, or putty beige. I like to look at them from my seat in the square and imagine what their view is like. I know that short of a lightning strike of a lottery win, nothing in my life will enable me to own one of these houses. I have always considered myself a lucky person, but I know it's not the kind of luck that manifests as period property with all the original features intact and the deeds in my name.

This is my favourite open public space in the city. Pond Square is also well loved by the owners of the houses that encircle it, some of whom have campaigned in the past for it to be gated and sealed off from the public. But that hasn't happened yet, and in the meantime it is somewhere I come to sit on a hot day. The pillars of the tree trunks, and the dim sunlight that filters down through their leaves, give the space the airy grandeur of a Great Hall in an old Victorian museum or institution. The breeze under the branches makes it cooler here on a hot day than it is in the flat that I rent down the road.

* * *

Before I moved to London, I visited. I came to prime the city, to prepare for my own time here, and I stayed with one friend or another, girls I'd worked or studied with who had made the journey here on the ferry ahead of me. They had jobs in bars and unpaid internships or were about to do a masters. They tended to live in flatshares in east London, and I would spend a night or two, crowded into a standard double bed alongside my friend. I still lived at home then, like many students in Ireland who go to university in the same place they grow up, and at home my own books and magazines and beauty products lay scattered around my childhood bedroom.

On these visits, I was agog at the way my friends had created a home of their own in an entirely new place. In one there was the Primark bed linen and the inherited knick-knacks that crowded the cabinet, itself found on the side of the street around the corner. Another home would be marked by the vintage dresses draped over the back of a chair, and the leather combat boots on the floor beside. There was also the smell of these flats, which I considered to be the distillation of 'London flat', so that if I read a book or watched a film afterwards where the character lives in a London flat, it was the smell of these flats that came to mind – soup cooking on the stove, wet umbrellas drying by the storage heater. In the mornings I watched these women prepare their breakfast before they left to go to work, the way one would spoon out yoghurt and granola with care, mixing until she achieved the right consistency, or how another would spread a decadent wedge of butter on toast. In these objects and actions I saw adult life as it was waiting for me after university. It was independence as I had not been able to access for myself before then.

Then I'd watch as my friend would put on her coat and her combat boots, give me the spare key, and leave for her shift. I would be alone with just the directions to the Tube station and a flimsy idea of where I might go for lunch, on her recommendation. As I got myself together and took a last look at her flat before setting out, I felt a pang in my chest – an almost romantic yearning for the life she'd carefully made for herself.

* * *

I am sure that other flats exist at cheaper prices, in other parts of the city. But unfortunately, this is where I feel most at home, which means I am stuck. The travel writer Jonathan Raban, who similarly found himself living on the side of Highgate Hill, in the late 1960s, wrote of the discrepancy between the summit of the hill and the bottom of it:

> Up on the crest of the hill, one is in the world of the for-ever fading glory of sober, middle-class prosperity. Down in the thick chemical air of the ravine, one is in the quick-penny land of used car dealers, betting shops, grave Irish bar-loungers, and men who stop you in the street with offers of second-hand shirts.

Since the 1970s, when Raban was writing, London's property market has undergone a shift. Now there are no quick-penny pockets of central London, including Archway, the ravine of which he writes. In any area of the city as far as Zone 3 or 4 a family home will be out of reach of first-time buyers on the median salary. On the median salary, its purchase will neces-sitate the kind of lump sum that usually comes with genera-tional wealth. I do not have such a lump sum, and so I rent along with the other millions of tenants in the city, forking out hundreds of pounds each and every month to ensure my landlord has enough money to hand down to his own chil-dren someday.

I signed a lease on this latest flat, my sixth home in London, ten years after I first visited my friends' flatshares. By some small miracle it is not much more expensive than any other similar flat in less leafy areas of the city. This flat is on the top floor of an old building that sits on the side of the hill. The kitchen has a small square window over the sink – the best place for a kitchen window – and through it there is a view of the splayed-out city, miles and miles of development out to the east. I wash my dishes in the evening and look out, thinking of the girl in the film who moves to the city to begin her life, and starts by gazing out at the city lights. Or the detective who comes home to his house on the side of the hill and stares out, puzzling through the dead-end of his case. Or the lovers who drive up the side of the hill to make their move. A view like this is cinematic, which is perhaps why it is also expensive – because often the cinematic is confused with the rarefied, and thus expensive. Looking at the view from the kitchen sink, I try to remember that sometimes the most cinematic elements of life are also the cheap and tawdry stuff, the parts of life without a price tag at all.

At the other end of the new flat, there is a full-length window looking out onto the street, and the curve of the road outside means that I have an excellent view of the grocery delivery vans on their rounds, and the vintage sports cars parked around the corner, and of passers-by as they walk – and they of me. For some reason, I seem to be condemned to live in flats like this in London – in buildings where passers-by pause to point up at us, murmuring something I can't hear into the ear of their companion. Maybe it's because I allow the pretty exterior picture on the estate agent website to guide me. 'Ooh, the architecture,' I coo, mentally doing the algebra that allows me to accept living in a flat with no oven, or no bath, or no internal storage. *But the architecture is so unique.* Of course, there was one flat where they pointed because the house looked so dilapidated. I did some research into that house and found the character appraisal documents, where the council examines the neighbourhood's status as designated conservation area. 'Unfortunately,' the text read, 'the poor condition of number 13's front elevation detracts from the character of the street.'

It was not my fault that the Victorian house was falling down. There were rats in the walls of that building long before I got there, and when there was a strong breeze it rattled the curtains and sent a ghostly shiver down everyone's spine. I could do nothing about the windows. But it was my fault for choosing to live there in the first place. I thought it was a bargain. I thought that the space and the light and the pretty Victorian character of the street would be enough to redeem it for me. In the end I hated living there, hated in particular the wealthy neighbours who ignored me when I said hello to them, because they had seen me coming out of the falling-down house and had drawn their own conclusions about me, too.

Now I have lived in London long enough to know that the extra hundred pounds in rent, if it can be swung, is worth it if it saves you the problems of rodents and cold and damp and troubles with the electrics. It took a long time for me to find myself with the extra hundred pounds, though. For years I felt I was looking at a balance sheet that I couldn't quite make add up. I changed my priorities in line with this reality and tried to shift my career so that it would give me more financial stability. What I am trying to say is that money is the reason for almost every decision I have ever made in the city.

Money and desire, time and space. How these things overlap and influence one another. It explains why I live where I do, lie awake at night listening to either rodent noises in the walls or the silence of a peaceful street. Money is what makes me take a job or leave it, working in one company or on one contract just long enough to save enough to buy the time I need to write at home on my own – to write this book, for instance. It might not allow me to buy a house in Pond Square, but for now it allows me to rent not too far away. The ledger I keep in my head accounts for every decision I make in London: where in the city I live and work. Whether I buy the nice bottle of wine or stop in the corner shop to get a can of Carlsberg instead. If I am eating vegetarian at home this week, or if I've booked a table at Noble Rot where I'll meet my friends and chat nonsense for several hours over expensive Spanish anchovies and bone-dry Austrian wine.

Money is also what makes me dress the way I do. When I can afford it, I go to the hairdresser every eight weeks for a cut. When I can't, I trim my fringe unevenly over the bathroom sink and let the rest grow scraggly around my shoulders.

I feel self-conscious walking around the city, wearing my bank balance on my head. But of course, nobody else makes the connection between my hair and my wallet. Instead, clothes and grooming and all our well-kept surfaces are often taken as evidence of style or good taste. Perhaps it's too easy to confuse money with good taste. I certainly have found myself confused. It is all too easy to look at some beautiful and well-presented woman on the street or on the internet and think: she knows exactly what she is doing. I too would like to know what I am doing, like her.

What she is doing, of course, is having money, probably lots of it, enough that she doesn't have to worry about where the next lot of money will come from.

There is a period in my twenties when I think that more money will be the answer, even when I am not sure of the question. When money is scarce, and the things I want to own cost so much, it seems likely that more money may even make me happy. Then, quite suddenly, after a brief and mild illness, I develop a kind of agoraphobia that renders me useless, and I start spending all my savings on private therapy. It is £60 for fifty minutes and, sitting tearful in my therapist's well-appointed room, I can almost feel the money draining out of my bank account. I can almost hear it: all the pints I turned down, the dinners where I skipped a starter and a dessert, and the taxis I forwent in favour of the long night bus home. The black leather boots I didn't buy, even though they were on deep discount in the sale. I can hear the sound of them clacking down streets without me. All the pounds I moved diligently into a separate account, all in the hope I might eventually buy a home of my own, all now paying for me to cry in a stranger's basement, in her nice house in Camden Town.

It's worth it, of course, because the therapy allows me slowly to redevelop a sense of self and enables me to restart my rambling around the city. The months I spent afraid of the street ebb away in my memory and after I say goodbye to my therapist, who proclaims me cured, the period of fear seems almost like a fever dream.

The sums, however, have always felt concrete. The numbers might go up and down from month to month, but the reality of them is always the same. I have thought about it at length and am aware of no potential change to my personal circumstances that would by now enable me to purchase and live in one of the pleasant old houses that overlook Pond Square. Not to worry: they rarely come on the market, anyway. Outside my new flat, children in smart uniforms walk to school in the mornings. It is some months before I learn, from an article in the newspaper, that the local schools cost over £20,000 a year: that each of those children's uniforms represents a number that is a healthy proportion of my own annual income.

There is an injustice that I feel when confronted with the numbers, as well as what they represent: choices that not everyone gets to make. The well-off couples who can have babies at whatever age they choose, knowing there will be enough money to feed and clothe and educate them in perpetuity, whatever happens. The minimalists who espouse chucking everything out because it's easy to replace anything when you have deep pockets. The people mistaken for chic, when really all that means is that they can afford a home with internal storage, so their living rooms are less cluttered than my own. I buy a console table from a seller on Gumtree for £15 and go to collect it. The address brings me to a double-fronted detached house with a sprawling garden and basement conversion. I am greeted by a man my own age who takes the £15 cash from me in exchange for the battered second-hand table, which I lug home and up two flights of stairs. When the console table is in my hallway and I have got my breath back, I can't help myself. I look up the house online and find it is worth over £3 million.

The numbers could drive me demented, but I try not to let them. Anyway, I know I am lucky to live in a nice neighbourhood, lucky to have the time and freedom to linger on the bench in Pond Square on a hot afternoon and to write this book when I get home. I know this to be true, yet still I worry about the sums. I run calculations constantly in order to find slightly better ways to live. I stop going to in-person yoga classes in favour of a more cost-effective option, streaming yoga videos from my mat on the living room floor. 'Find your edge and get comfortable there,' the lithe woman on my phone screen tells me as I settle into sleeping pigeon pose. Now I am thinking about money again, thinking about how this is the way I operate with earning money, too: find my edge, the point at which I can work enough to get by, and then retreat. What would it be to break with this habit? What would it take to learn to live in a different way?

Years ago, when I was in the middle of the agoraphobia that led me to all that therapy, I was in the car with my dad and I asked him if he worried about things a lot. If he was a person who worried the way that I did.

'I used to be,' he said. He said he used to worry so much, all the time, about money. He worried he didn't have enough, he wasn't earning enough, he wouldn't be able to take care of our family in the way he wanted to.

'And then,' he said, rubbing his chin, 'in my forties, I thought about it and how pointless it was, and one day I decided to stop. And I stopped worrying.'

12. On the Hampstead Heath Extension

It's December, and in London the daylight has gone on annual leave. Nonetheless here I am, beating muddy paths across Hampstead Heath every morning before work to rehabilitate my chest, battered by a bout of Covid.

I am trying, on these walks, to make sense of the year. Probably a fruitless task, but anyway. On we go. Is 2020 the year of disappointment? A year of isolation, but also, of a strange new commonality. The year I became overly attached to the hyperlocal milieu: the sight of the tree surgeons, the postmen, the greengrocer. The elderly woman in the fleece practising her little ukulele in the rain in the park. The athletic young man who strings his gymnastic rings from the sturdy branch of a beech tree and hoists himself up. The year we all entered a waiting room and silently took a seat, kept glancing at the wall where the clock should rightfully be and finding nothing. The only realisation I can draw is that all of it counted. None of it is wasted, even if it didn't go as we wished it would. Even if it felt like nothing more than marking time. Even marking time is still life lived, months or years of my own life – a thought I am sometimes scared by and sometimes find exhilarating.

I wish I could say something like: looking at strangers in the way I write about has been a solace through all of this. But even the loose and casual interactions that living in the world provides are frayed now. The year has been a long exercise in disconnection from other people. It is something I try to push against, and often fail.

Every year, at this dark point in the calendar, the pleasure or pain of strangers can start to feel unusually close. It can start to feel like my own pleasure or pain. A man driving a supermarket delivery van is blaring Stevie Wonder, reversing out of a driveway. I pause to let him past and smile at his enjoyment of the music – a mistake, as he then rolls down his window and makes a lewd gesture at me. Further on, over-prepared dog walkers in quilted liners and sou'westers. Couples in hiking boots having difficult conversations. Teen-agers who climb the muddy high bank of the pond, extending an arm to take a selfie. A mother and daughter cut from the same cloth, both with long curly hair and white and neon trainers. An older runner passes me, a tall plastic hood protecting his Sikh turban from the rain. All of it feels very

close to the surface. I know that if I want, I can put my headphones on, pull the hood of my raincoat up, hunch my shoulders and try to blot out the rest of the world. Instead, I turn
outwards. I tilt my face up to face the rain and for a second,
I close my eyes.

FIELD NOTES
WINTER

Marylebone High Street

A woman in the softest, fluffiest pink faux fur coat – the fur long and feathery, and so she looks like an excessively groomed Afghan hound, or a hairy egg. I try to think of what kind of animal might possibly produce a fur like this, but there is none.

In the Eurostar departures lounge in St Pancras station

Three petite students in huge down jackets and face masks, the quilted technical fabric rustling as they push rolling metallic luggage towards the escalator.

The coffee shop in Vauxhall

The tattooed barista with the moustache wipes down his espresso machine slowly and lovingly between uses, despite the lengthy queue forming outside.

At the bar at the Royal Opera House

An elegant woman in her eighties, dressed in floor-grazing crimson velvet, belted at the waist with something sparkly. Carrying a full-sized umbrella in one hand and a glass of champagne in the other.

A small playground in Tufnell Park

'I asked you a question,' the man in the forest-green gilet says to his curly-haired toddler in oatmeal overalls, who is on one of those little tricycles. 'And you didn't know the answer, because you were looking in the wrong direction.'

Crossing Oxford Circus

A woman in an expensive cream coat with a single brown plait hanging to her waist, thick as a horse's mane, pushes a stately black Balmoral pram.

Holland Park

Two goths on a date. Matching long black leather coats, Dr. Martens and black backpacks. Both with long dark hair, giving an androgynous vibe to the pair. Something that looks suspiciously like a riding crop poking out of the taller one's bag.

A red-bricked street off Camberwell Road

A food delivery driver clad in Kardashian-grade black spandex, a single long hot-pink plait dangling from under her helmet.

The up escalator at Camden Town station
A heavily tattooed man in a neon yellow fleece. As he passes me, I can see the back of it is embroidered with the words *LOVE ME OR LEAVE ME*.

Old Compton Street
A waiter in a worn yet sophisticated waistcoat over a white shirt, dipping out to the covered outdoor seating in a rainstorm. A beleaguered look on his face.

Near the men's bathing pond on Hampstead Heath
Man with grey hair and colourful socks, tramping resolutely on the backs of his shoes as he walks home from his swim in the rain – mud splattering everywhere with each step, but he does seem to be content.

Jermaine Francis

Photographer

You've recently published a book called *Rhythms from the Metroplex*, the latest in a series of personal projects that are taken from the city and the street.

It's a weird thing. I'd been reading Henri Lefebvre's *Rhythmanalysis*, and had been working for years on a series of photos about the rhythm of the city. I was trying to figure it out. I got to this point where I knew what made sense in it. And then the pandemic hit. So obviously that was out the window.

Instead, you started going out on these lockdown walks around London with your camera. These became another book, called *Something That Seemed So Familiar Becomes Distant*.

I had an intention in some way, even if I didn't know what would happen. I was thinking the photos would be about space, distance, how we read the space. Strange, everyday objects, and people. I wouldn't see anybody on the street, and then I'd see a key worker, or lots of people in masks. But stuff was still going on, things were still happening. You'd see police cordons, and gangs were still very active, graffiti was appearing more and more. The streets were empty, but not silent. Where I live in north London, there's a lot of green space in the estates. I realised how those green spaces became so important for the people who lived in those flats.

So after you made a book of those images, you then went back to those pre-pandemic photos of the city and people on the streets.

Rhythms from the Metroplex was about how people interact in the city and how we move. Also it was about these narratives in the city which exist in the everyday, and about looking and observing. So it was looking at all these different interactions going on in the city, in crowds, and what I started to notice, looking back at those pictures, were these patterns, these stories.

Where did you go to take these photos?

One example is that I went to Bank at rush hour. And I was intrigued by how in some ways, people are just like worker bees, going to work. Interaction with each other is very minimal, Bank is a space for passing through, to get to a place of commerce. And how packed it was, with people trying to weave in and out. But there was also something else going on in that scene – the newspaper vendor. Do you know the history of the newspaper vendor in London?

No.

So the *Evening Standard* vendors had historically been self-employed – you owned your plot on a particular street, and it was passed down generation to generation. The vendors would make money from the sales of the paper, and their customers would see them every day, talk to them, 'How are you? What's going on?' They had a position within the capitalist structure.

Then around the time that the *Evening Standard* decided it would go free [in 2009], the paper decided that the vendors had to be on a payroll instead. It totally transformed the economics of their labour. Because the paper was free, they wouldn't be making money from each one. They were just paid a salary, and that was less than what they would have made when self-employed. And there was a completely different dynamic then, in the exchange between the workers going to work, and the vendor. I also noticed that today they wear hi-vis. In a city, hi-vis can give you a lot of freedom.

A hi-vis jacket gives you a kind of authority or status in a crowd, too.

Yeah, a sense of authority. It can mean responsibility, the freedom to go places and nobody will question what you're doing. But it's also a marker of your economic class, and in the case of the newspaper vendor, it can make people who had been visible very invisible in a way. This person who is a vendor is being ignored constantly by the people around them. Those people can see him, but it's almost like he doesn't exist, they're just barging past. There's a bittersweet moment in my series where a woman does actually take a newspaper. Now, she's not buying it, she's taking it, it's free. And the vendor is looking in the opposite direction.

You mentioned that you're interested in the act of observing in the city. How did you explore that in these images?

There was one moment while I was making *Rhythms from the Metroplex*. I was in Oxford Circus, taking photos. That area's prime time for street photographers, which is one of the reasons I was there.

So I'm taking pictures. At one point I see the police, and suddenly I notice one of them starts approaching me from across the road. He calls me, and I'm thinking maybe it's because I photographed them, since they're in the general space. And he says, 'Excuse me, can I look at what's on your camera?' I show him and he says, 'You seem to have a few photographs of me.'

I say, 'Well, yes, because you're in the space that I'm photographing, so you probably will be. But if you want me to delete it, I'm more than happy if you don't want to be in any of these images.'

He says. 'No, no, I don't have a problem. So, what are you doing?'

I say, [deadpan] 'I'm taking photographs.'

And he replies, 'That's really strange, isn't it. A really strange thing to be doing, don't you think? Why are you doing that?'

I say, 'Well, I make projects, I'm a photographer.' I knew instantly what was going on. They were questioning me about my behaviour. So we get into the conversation, and I basically decide to just cut the crap. I go: 'This is who I am,' and I show him my Instagram, which is the easiest thing to do. At that time I'd had a photograph in the National Portrait Gallery.

'So,' I say, 'can I ask you, why are you questioning me? Let's just cut the dance.'

'Well, we're questioning you because you've been reported, and we thought you might be a terrorist.'

'OK,' I say, 'so who called it in and what was the description?'

And I'll never do this again – that day, I'd left my Berghaus jacket at home because it was dirty, I'd put it in the wash. And instead I'd put on my military jacket, because it was December, and I thought, that'll be warm enough. I had that on with a baseball cap. And the policeman says, 'Well, you were reported because you're wearing a military jacket, a camouflage jacket.'

I say, 'Also, you left out a bit of the description, haven't you? Because I know that the person reporting is going to have described me, too. And I'm Black.' And I saw his face change, like he was saying yes. And I knew I'd been socially profiled by the police. There were other photographers around, and they weren't being questioned in the same way.

Did that interaction affect how you felt about your freedom to move around, your freedom to take photos of what you want in the city?

It did throw me off a bit. I've been aware of these things in relation to photography since I was at university, when I realised that the American road trip, which is sort of a rite of passage in photographic history, is something that I would never be able to do, because of racism. That's the thing I thought about when taking these photographs – I wouldn't say I'm taking risks, but I am exposing myself to certain elements. That's something that I always think about. It's similar with women on the street, female photographers. They're exposing themselves in some situations. I always know I'm Black, I've been through it before, but there's a sense that when you're taking photos, doing something you enjoy, that this is a consideration that other people don't have to take on board, when they go and make a picture. But I do. I'm aware of my surroundings at all times, in certain situations. In a way this book is sort of like a road trip of my own across London, and in the end I included those photos with the police officers, that whole interaction, in the book, because that's the thing about space that I was trying to investigate: that I'm a photographer, I'm observing people, and then suddenly I become the observed, too.

13. At Oxford Circus

A prematurely sunny spring day in Marylebone, and I'm waiting outside the supermarket, wafting the sides of my green woollen coat open to let the cool air in. Across the road the sunlight is hitting the handsome flats above the line of shops; in one window, I see a hand reach up and tug the curtains across to block the light. I realise at once how the same thing that delights me down here can frustrate up there, all down to a change of the angle. I imagine the person up there in the small room over the high street, the light dazzling her view of the laptop, as she sits at the folding table beside her bed.

Meanwhile, back at street level, there are three taxi cabs beside me in single file at the kerb. They are waiting hopefully for fares to emerge from the supermarket's automatic doors. There are no fares around anymore. 'Death row,' I hear one of the drivers say as he hops out of the front seat to chat to the others. They stand near the taxis, not leaning on them, and I take their posture to be a sign of respect for the cabs, which are elegant, gleaming in the bright sun. The streets are quiet now in the final days of this long lockdown, and the driver says he'll probably just sit here on the high street until he clocks off in the late afternoon.

It has been a year of navigating the city in a new way, and what is most strange to me is that it still feels new. The novelty hasn't quite worn off. The first time I came to the new central London was a few weeks into the first lockdown, when I woke up early on a Sunday morning to put on my running shoes and jog directly into the heart of the city. Crossing from Regent's Park over Marylebone Road triggered a kind of awe that increased as I got further south. The city, its very beating heart that I knew so well, was empty.

The archetypal city scene, pedestrians striding across the five-way scramble intersection at Oxford Circus with such determination – all gone. No buses now, and only the odd car. And nobody else around barring me and two cyclists, all of us turning incredulous loops in the middle of the road, cameras held aloft in some blank reverie.

My friend Stevie once interviewed a priest for a podcast we did together about clothes, and the priest said that he was careful never to break into a run while in his clerical clothing, even if he saw his bus zooming towards his bus stop ahead of him. People don't like to see a running priest, he said. They think something terrible must have happened, if a priest is running. I was reminded of this when I saw Oxford Circus turned inside-out in this way. My mind can't access a middle ground: it goes immediately to zombie films, the dystopias from science fiction, because these are the only places I've seen city streets rendered like this. Something terrible must have happened, I thought, if the city centre is devoid of people.

And quite obviously it had. I was here, running ten miles at 9 a.m. on a Sunday because there was a global pandemic underway and because I had nothing else to do with my free time. At this point thousands had died and many more had been made ill. A sense of utter uncertainty, the depths of which I have never known in my own lifetime, filled the space we'd vacated by staying at home.

At this same time, photos circulated online, like the ones I took on my phone that morning at Oxford Circus. We were all collectively astonished, it seemed, to see these familiar scenes so depleted. The Eiffel Tower, or Times Square – there is something uncanny and compelling about it. Something tells me, when I look at these images, that I'm looking at a fake of some sort. I had always believed that people are a part of the place, and to confront the place without its people is a cognitive challenge. Any beauty that the images might contain is an eerie one.

But the emptiness was also a trick of the eye. Writing in the *Guardian* later in the year about photos of deserted cities under lockdown, the critic Sophie Haigney writes that the images were 'an exercise in myth-making', an attempt to establish a narrative of hope. The images of empty cities that proliferated in those early days were an attempt to prove that people everywhere, all over the world, were coming together in the battle against the spread of the virus. In the face of an uncontrollable pandemic, cities elected to empty themselves out. But, Haigney points out, 'the world only ever looked unpeopled from certain vantage points'. While many stayed at home, many others couldn't. 'Life for many people didn't come to a full stop; it simply became more dangerous,' she writes.

All photos are tricks of the eye in one way or another. They are versions of reality that show the subject from only one angle, and the viewer tends to fill in the rest for themselves. This is what I saw in empty Oxford Circus: shuttered shops, electronic window displays still blinking. Abandoned roadworks. Flashing signs at the entrances to the Tube reading *Stay Alert >> Control the Virus*. And pavements with no shoppers, no tourists, no homeless people, no commuters. Just me and a couple of others, who wandered out early on a Sunday morning to see what it was like out there.

Months later on, the city again in lockdown, I go out on the street in a different way. At home on my laptop, cross-legged on my bed, I trawl through the online archives of various London street photographers. After the Second World War, Henry Grant worked for most of his life as a freelance photographer for a Fleet Street news agency. Grant was a socialist, and often collaborated with his journalist wife Rose in her coverage for the communist newspaper the *Daily Worker* (publishing today as the *Morning Star*), among others. For almost forty years he photographed life in the city from every imaginable angle, and in the 1980s the Museum of London bought his entire archive of around 80,000 black and white photos.

I comb through Grant's archives from my bed. It is winter, and the virus is raging through the country once again. I am looking for the city in its quotidian normality, and I find it in photographs from the 1950s onwards. Children dressed up for coronation street parties. A nun in a crisp white cornette hat, waiting on a train platform at King's Cross station. Town hall weddings. Dancers backstage at the Royal Ballet School. A crowd of shoppers, gathered to watch a one-man band on the street in Camden. A man sits with a cup of coffee in the window of Patisserie Valerie on Old Compton Street. A tradesman replacing caning on battered old chairs, sitting on the pavement while he works. Well-heeled visitors looking at the Parthenon sculptures at the British Museum. Firefighters on strike. Children at rent protests. Anti-Nazi gatherings in Trafalgar Square. Traders on the floor of the London Stock Exchange.

Grant's archive is huge, city-sized in its own way. As soon as I leaf past one photograph it takes on a hazy allure in my mind, like a street I once walked on and soon forgot about. Grant's work for the newspapers means that many of his photographs contain some newsworthy event. But there are many more images of ordinary life in the city – the stuff that doesn't make it to the papers – and I think these have a historic kind of depth to them, too. Through the archives, a thread of progress can be traced. New buildings, new technologies, new advertisements, vehicles, products to purchase. But Londoners remain at the heart of Grant's work throughout: their ordinary, everyday lives are the one constant as all else changes.

I am reminded of how much of life can play out on the street. In one image, a child is treated by some kind of podiatrist at what the caption says is a 'makeshift foot clinic', among the stalls at Chapel Street market. In another, a well-dressed man and woman both lounge, possibly dozing, on the steps of the University of London. Sometimes, Grant's focus is on a single person, caught off guard as they peer into a shop window. Sometimes his sense of scale is much greater: the faces of Londoners filling every inch of Trafalgar Square for an anti-apartheid protest in the early 1960s. That's the true experience of the everyday city, really, and what I miss most under lockdown: that within seconds I can go from feeling entirely alone, singular, like a character in a movie, to feeling part of humanity, inextricable and indistinguishable from my fellow Londoners past and present.

It is a thrill when I recognise a particular street in Grant's photos, even when the buildings have long since changed. The way the light falls on the nun's brilliant white cornette at

King's Cross station reminds me of one hundred scenes from movies that take place on train platforms, and it also reminds me of blurred scenes from my own life, boring hours spent waiting for trains. Grant having captured this moment in a photograph is what makes it more notable, even in its ordinariness. Photographs like these are a way to imagine, and a way to remember.

Born in London to Irish parents, I was six when we returned to Ireland. Growing up in Ireland, my memories of earliest childhood in London quickly coalesced into a series of hazy images. Some of these rested on actual family photographs that I could revisit over and over, until the photograph itself supplanted the memory.

I remember sitting on my dad's shoulders watching the Chinese New Year festivities at Gerrard Place, watching the dragon dance and feeling confused. It was a dragon, with a fearsome face, and yet it had human legs, legs that wore jeans and trousers like everyone else.

I remember also being taken to Notting Hill Carnival, which was the first and possibly only time I ever saw someone wearing a 'foam dome' drinking hat. The feeling of being in a crowd, being small amid the bulk of bodies that make up the crowd itself – this was something that did not start to scare me until much later in life.

I remember trips to Kew Gardens and the zoo at Regent's Park. I remember dropping something small – a stone or a bead – onto the train tracks at Kew Gardens station, and being prevented immediately from reaching down to get it. For the longest time I remembered standing on the bridge at the Regent's Canal, just by the entrance to London Zoo, and looking down to see hippos and crocodiles in the water, though that memory was of course a little confused.

Or it's possible that I don't remember any of these days so much as I remember the photographs, some of which are framed on the walls of my family home, some in big A3 scrapbooks with captions and dates scribbled in blue biro underneath.

I liked growing up and studying in Dublin. It is a real city, though maybe not a true metropolis. While I lived there I enjoyed the dual sensations of which a city of its size is capable: the usual pushing through a crowded bar at a concert or play, walking down Grafton Street amid the throngs of pedestrians every morning, an endless parade of new faces. But I also loved the many times that the city felt more like a village – bumping into any number of acquaintances while going for a coffee, the ease of visiting friends in their homes, or seeing public figures do ordinary things like cycle along the river or collect their children from school.

Perhaps I took this sort of dual feeling for granted. While I was growing up and studying in Dublin, I yearned towards what was out there: the bigger city, London. The urban sprawl across the sea, nearly impossible to ignore with its long shadow often impacting life in Dublin, whether through politics at Westminster, or simply by absorbing your friends as they moved there to look for work.

I yearned towards the city through images, more than anything else. I had been there – had even lived there – but it was through photographs I'd seen in newspapers or magazines or found on the internet that I formed an idea of what life in London could be like for me.

In my teens, on the internet, I found that you could walk the streets of almost any city through the images taken by others. When I was at university, I would go to the computers that lined the concrete walls of the Arts Block, the ones on high desks without seats, and navigate to various fashion blogs. My favourites were the ones with posts consisting only of snapshots of well-dressed pedestrians in distant cities – Krakow, Oslo, Milan. No words other than the name of the street and the date, followed by photo after photo of people on the street, in their stylish outfits. Street-style blogs, in their fleeting late 2000s incarnation, were a pure distillation of so much that I wanted from life – simple days in a city that seemed chicer and more interesting solely because it wasn't the one I'd grown up in. It was a pure, imaginary kind of yearning, the same thing that drives some people to pack up their life and move to a new place in the belief it will cure their melancholy. Standing at the university computers, I could picture a life of my own, just a few short years away: me on my ladies pushbike in my elegant trench coat, a brown leather Louis Vuitton handbag casually worn cross-body or else sitting in my basket. A sharp haircut. A low heel. A coat of dark lipstick.

This version of me was more elegant, more polished, but was not a million miles from the version of myself I already embodied. But it was desirable because it hadn't happened yet, or maybe simply because it was already happening to other people in photographs, on the internet.

What was wrong with the life I was already living? Nothing in particular, other than that it was my life and that I had the sense peculiar to many people in their early twenties who are still living where they grew up, who believe deeply that somewhere there is something else out there, waiting for them. For me, that sense took its form in clothes and, most of all, in the clothes of other people – not celebrities or style icons, but the anonymous ordinary people I saw on blogs.

There were other blogs, too, where the people I looked at were not anonymous. I had one of these myself, using a self-timer camera to take pictures in my parents' kitchen, usually wearing a mix of vintage clothing and new items I'd got through my job at a trendy chain store on the high street. I enjoyed doing this – it gave me an outlet to think about clothing in a new light, and I made friendships with other young women from all over the world living all sorts of lives. But in those years that I had a fashion blog and religiously read thirty or forty others, the role of the blogger morphed drastically. Every blog post became a potential advertising hoarding, a space to rent for fashion brands

interested in finding audiences outside of magazines or billboards. Bloggers themselves, especially if they were pretty
enough and thin enough, could easily become paid clothes
horses. The potential for profit was a powerful fuel for many
bloggers, who could happily mould themselves into whatever
shape was necessary to generate an income through affiliate
links and gifted items.

From my perch at the university computer I watched
peers become full-time bloggers, in receipt of a steady stream
of revenue, which meant they could keep broadcasting their
desirable, aspirational life to their readers. I wondered if
there was something wrong with me, that I didn't want to
do this with my own image. I thought about building a brand
through my blog and shuddered, starting to turn away from
the whole thing. What had started as an obsessive interest in
high fashion, coupled with a sort of delirious love of getting
dressed, had petered out once bottom lines came into it. By
the time I moved to London I had developed other outlets
for my love of fashion, outside of the personal blog.

Street-style blogs were changing, too. The race for profit
meant that the photographers who used to roam various
cities, looking for stylish strangers, were now focusing
their gaze solely on fashion weeks attended by industry
people – editors and stylists and models often paid to wear
the designer clothes they were photographed in. In quick
time this paradigm ate itself. And it wasn't interesting to me

anymore. There was no magic in seeing a stylist or a model – whoever they were, they were usually tall and thin and beautiful and rich – with access to any amount of beautiful items of clothing, wearing a full look straight from a Dior ad campaign. Where was the delirious magic of getting dressed?

In 2013, the fashion critic Suzy Menkes wrote an incendiary article for the *New York Times* about the phenomenon of 'clothes pegs' outside fashion shows. 'They pose and preen,' she wrote, 'in their multipatterned dresses, spidery legs balanced on club-sandwich platform shoes, or in thigh-high boots under sculptured coats blooming with flat flowers.'

I knew what she meant, even if my fellow fashion students and I thought she sounded a little elitist, a little out of touch. This was the fashion industry now, and it was a world I was stepping into myself. I attended these fashion shows, another nobody pressing through a crowd to get a look at the runway, and I watched the paparazzi scrum over whichever fashion editor or influencer was the dish of the day. I said to myself that it had nothing to do with what I was there for, which was to look at the new collections and then to write about them. But of course it did – it was a complex ecosystem, an exchange of power between photographer and subject and fashion brand. Gone were the creativity and the anonymity that had first captured my attention back in Dublin.

Why did any of this matter so much to me? Why did I care at all? Were they not just clothes, at the end of the day?

Maybe I had overestimated their importance in my own life, or certainly in the wider world – this was what I was told by young men I met at parties, who were shocked that someone who met their criteria for intelligence wrote about fashion for a living. But clothing was how I ascertained my identity. It is how many of us do that. It gave me a chance to figure out who I was, and who I wanted to be. And when I moved to London, clothing was the way I made sense of myself in a sprawling, unfamiliar new place. I was, in the way of all twenty-two-year-olds undergoing new experiences, finding new depths within myself, new dimensions and facets.

It wasn't that I could express myself through a given outfit, but that I could channel some of the raw energy of myself into how I dressed. There was nothing more honest to me than getting up in the morning and putting on something I loved to wear. To sully that process with commerce, money, profit – it felt like tearing down a beloved old historic building to put up a block of luxury flats in its place.

Despite the fact that this was the industry I now worked in – that in a way, I'd got what I had been striving for all along – I found it alienating, boring. I started to hate crowding into the basement venues and hotel ballrooms for fashion shows. I turned down the invites to parties because the parties were never fun. I turned back to the streets instead, and to my own body, my own dressed self. I looked at the city and, in this way, I found a way of looking at myself.

***

When the streets of the city began to fill up again, I started to take cautious steps back into normal urban life. I crossed the city to meet friends at restaurants. I met colleagues on park benches to talk about work. I shopped for lipsticks. Again and again I donned my mask and descended the escalator to the loathed Northern line. Quickly, it became difficult to remember what exactly this place had been like when it was empty. I walked along Hatton Garden with Karl, having just purchased two gold wedding bands. I pointed to the windows of the jewellers that lined the street and tried to explain to Karl how uncanny it had been to see them all empty back in January: row after row of black felt boxes, with nothing inside to dazzle and catch the eye.

On the bus home, I started to think about all the photographs of London again: the way I build and rebuild the city in my mind through the photos taken by others. In Henry Grant's photos of London, every ordinary person, every unexceptional event, is newsworthy in its way.

Susan Sontag wrote in *On Photography* that 'photographs shock insofar as they show something novel'. What was novel about the photographs of London's empty streets in the pandemic was the absence of people. For a brief time, I could see the backdrop of all the drama and mundanity of my life a little clearer. But now it is back to being mere backdrop. I pass through the streets once again, in the clothes I use to make myself who I am. I carry with me my own thoughts and desires, my internal monologues and my complex neuroses. I am the same, in so many ways, as everyone who walked these streets before me.

14. At Trafalgar Square

When I reach the top of the escalator, I see that the ticket hall of Leicester Square station is crowded with people. Shuffling in the direction of the exits, loitering near the ticket barriers – the space is dense with bodies and their chatter. I find a fast-moving current of people who have no interest in spending an extra second here and push myself into it. We cut through the melee to escape out to the street.

My heartbeat quickens as I climb the stairs, and when I reach street-level, it sees no reason to slow again: out on Charing Cross Road, the crowds are here too. It is a Saturday afternoon, and they are protesting something. It is hard to tell what exactly, but they have a look common to protesting crowds, a look that's both angry and jubilant. I can see that the crowd stretches far south, to the National Portrait Gallery and beyond, to Trafalgar Square. This, unfortunately, is the way I am headed.

In crowds like this, it's easier to see what Londoners have in common with one another, even if we don't think it. There are so many pairs of Nikes on the feet of those around me, for instance, all different kinds of people who have chosen the same brand of footwear, that they may as well be the official shoe brand of the city.

I walk down Charing Cross Road, hugging the outermost edge of the pavement. Quickly I begin to feel light-headed with it: the subtle loss of identity I experience whenever I slip into a crowd. There are two competing impulses at work within me, and both strike me as deeply human. One is to escape, and the other is to stay and soak it up. I think I fear the crowd, yet I also love it. It is possibly its power that scares me but that's probably also what I enjoy about it. When I am here, the power and potential become mine, too.

London is a place well acquainted with the crowd. Crowds are a constant that courses throughout life in the city. Not just the masses who fill Tube carriages and Oxford Street pavements, but protests and parties, too – crowds who take to the streets with purpose. The mob and its power have a lengthy history in this country, and where they go, the abstract fear of what they might achieve can follow close behind. People have been revolting here, against one thing or another, for centuries. In 1381, the Peasants' Revolt saw rebels from Kent and Essex pour into London in the summer months to protest against inequalities that had arisen during

the Hundred Years' War with France and in the years after
the Black Death. In particular, they wanted no further heavy
poll tax, and they were angry enough to demand the teenage
King's head, too. When they reached the city, the rebels
aimed their rage at what they saw as the heedless wealth of
the metropolis: palaces and homes of wealthy noblemen, the
law books held at Temple. In their fury they threw the furni-
ture and fittings of the Savoy Palace directly into the Thames.
The reaction from the Crown was swift and decisive. King
Richard II sent in his armies, and after some weeks the rebel-
lion was bloodily suppressed. The leaders of the revolt were
mostly executed, and any concessions granted by the King
in negotiations were later rescinded. But parliament did, at
least, stop trying to introduce a poll tax.

This was the first popular uprising in English history. The
lesson, if there was one, is that the crowd can be powerful,
and it can also be quashed.

In my time in London, the crowd has been less charged
than in previous eras. I arrived in the wake of the riots in
the summer of 2011, and there were still businesses with
broken windows near where I lived then in Mile End. The
November before, I'd sat in my parents' kitchen and watched
rolling news coverage of protests in the UK against university
tuition fees. The helicopter images shown were evocative: a
sea of young people in winter coats against the cold, playing
music, some climbing on monuments or traffic lights, waving

banners and flags, a heavy police presence, and eventually, kettling − cordons of police officers surrounding groups of students and preventing them from moving − which was also a direct way to scare away anyone who might want to join such a protest in the future.

Like all Londoners, I quickly became accustomed to the crowd once I moved here. It didn't take long to become inured to the sardine-tin squeeze of the rush hour Tube carriage, or the scrum crossing Oxford Circus once the lights change. I chose to spend weekend nights in packed basement clubs on Kingsland Road, shoulder to clammy shoulder at the bar. I would lose track of friends on the dancefloor, watch them get carried away on the tide of the crowd until just a head, then an arm, was visible through the crush. I enjoyed it, usually. The key was to forget about the fact of your own body: the fears and desires, the urge for control that you might carry inside it. Some people find this easier than others; those people tend to take more pleasure from their lives here, I've noticed.

Sometimes I'm capable of doing this, though it gets more difficult as I get older. It can be a thrill to join the crowd when there is something to celebrate. At Notting Hill Carnival, or at street parties in my own neighbourhood, I watch my fellow Londoners exorcise something from themselves with great pleasure. In her book *Dancing in the Streets*, Barbara Ehrenreich found that taking to the streets to express collective joy is an ancient habit that goes back thousands of years, across human civilisations. I can feel this at community street parties I've attended: sometimes ramshackle affairs consisting of hired stages and speakers, blind eyes turned by the local council to noise complaints and Controlled Drinking Zone enforcements. There's nothing complicated here, just loud music and cheap cans of beer, maybe something hot and tasty cooked at a stall and handed to you, wrapped in greasy paper. Why is what results so joyful? Is it a collective agreement we've made to have fun? Is it that everything we push down inside ourselves when we join the restrained crowd of the commute is finally allowed out? There is an exhaustion in my bones when I come home from a day among this more vociferous kind of crowd. It is a good kind of exhaustion, the kind that makes me happy to be alive, and when I go to bed that night my sleep is sound and thick.

Not all crowds are joyous or fraught. Elsewhere there are also endless opportunities for mundanity. There are interminable queues due to crowd control and bureaucracy. I queue outside the vaccine centre for my Covid vaccine; I queue in a snaking tunnel around the train station concourse to board a train to Glasgow. There are queues up the steps at the British Museum, held up by the security checks visitors are subject to on entry. For a while there are even queues outside supermarkets, the ultimate in mundane queueing. These queues can test the patience, of which I tend to have very little. They are supposedly an English phenomenon, though this assumes, in very English fashion, that humans in other parts of the world are fundamentally unruly and hence incapable of standing in a line. Boring queues like these are no place for beauty or curiosity; in this country, in fact, I've found that it's almost rude to acknowledge the presence of others in a bureaucratic queue. We are all here to accomplish whatever it is the queue brings us to, and nothing more.

I pass the Garrick Theatre and I can see the protest march is starting to thin. There are still some stragglers, and some police officers, and the pavements are busy enough that it's still a struggle for me to make a path through. There is enough going on that I am still on guard in their presence, my tote bag clutched tightly underneath one arm. What is it that I dislike about being in the crowd? Perhaps it's the loss of control, the relinquishing of my own fears and desires for those of the people around me. In the right humour I can go with it. In the wrong humour it makes me second-guess my decision to live here. Could I not have chosen a smaller city, I plead with myself when, say, I join an escalator snake that goes down into the bowels of Moorgate station – a Stockholm or a Dublin? Might I enjoy my life more, if I gave my body more space from other people?

Sigmund Freud wrote that the individual who joins a crowd is giving up their own autonomy in favour of adopting a mass mindset. A kind of love for humanity forces us to surrender our own emotions in exchange for the emotions of the crowd. This is how crowds and mobs can turn civilised people into thugs or barbarians. Usually the crowd self-regulates:

on the Tube, Londoners know to stand on the right, to avoid talking to each other unless strictly necessary. Sometimes I still see individuals act with rampant self-interest, of course: barging the train doors as they close and holding up the service for everyone, being rude to their fellow passengers, eating or drinking or singing or shouting. But these individuals are usually met with a focused, quiet distaste from the rest of us. The rest of us, subtly or otherwise, give social cues that tell these people that their actions are not welcome here.

Now I reach the north-east corner of Trafalgar Square, where I'm early to meet a friend. Here is the tail end of the protest. The crowd hasn't come to a stop, exactly, but rather its solidity is disintegrating into smaller clusters made of tourists, shoppers, buskers, street performers in elaborate costume like forgotten movie props, friends meeting on the steps that overlook the fountains. I stand at the top of the square, with my back to the grand façade of the National Gallery. From here the masses seem further away, and I can feel my place among them more clearly. At the fringe of the protest, I can see a woman peeling off. She hugs a friend goodbye and then withdraws. As she walks away, I see her becoming herself again, more distinct. She is wearing a blue denim coat and a cream turtleneck, and is carrying a bright red tote bag. I watch her cross the road and step onto the stone of the square. For a few moments she is newly visible – she reaches up to run a hand through her hair, adjusting an earring on the way – and then she disappears. I lose sight of her in the throng of people on Trafalgar Square, all of them watching buskers, standing around and chatting or just passing through. I have a feeling, then, not unlike that of volume being turned down, having been at an insufferable level, and now leaving you with just a faint ringing in the ears.

Sofia Abdel-Nabi and Lizge Arslan

Students, both sixteen years old

Do you guys like fashion?

L: Yeah, my mum was a pattern cutter. So she worked with – I forgot the name of the brand, but she stitched their stuff together.

So did you grow up with sewing machines around?

L: We had one. It's broken, sadly!

Can you sew yourself?

L: Yeah. There was a whole period when I was younger where I got obsessed with sewing machines and making dresses for my dolls.

S: I quite like fashion, but not to that extent. I'm quite a shopaholic, I just shop a lot and spend a lot on fashion and clothes and stuff.

Do you shop online or do you go to a specific part of town?

S: Well, because of Covid I was doing a lot online. But I like to go and try stuff on. Because you don't know what it's going to look like in person.

It's really hard to see how the fabric's going to feel in a picture. Where do you like to go?

S: Oxford Street, because there's a variety of shops. And also Shein is quite good, online.

Were you excited when the shops reopened after lockdown?

Both: Yeah.

L: We went the first day they reopened.

S: We bought some stuff.

S: I got a skirt from Zara. Or I think it was a dress. But I took it back.

L: We went into Primark as well. The queue was massive. What did we get? I think we got like, a bikini. Because we knew it was going to get warm, so . . .

S: Yeah, we did both get bikinis.

Do you have to wear a uniform for school?

Both: No.

Did you have one before, when you were younger?

S: I did in primary school, so it was a massive change when I came [to secondary school]. I was like, 'Oh, I get so much freedom now.'

Were you happy about that?

S: Yeah, but after a while it gets so hard. Because you constantly think about what you have to wear.

Is there pressure in your school to have a good outfit, or to wear new things?

S: Not really. Some people roll up in pyjamas, no one really cares.

What is an outfit that you really love wearing?

L: Flared jeans. With usually any top, but something nice. I quite like plain tops. I'll pair it with another thing and add accessories. Like, you turn it into something nicer.

What do you like about flared jeans?

L: I like the way they proportion out your body. I've gone totally off skinny jeans, I prefer stuff that either goes out at the bottom or is quite baggy. That happened during lockdown, when I started doing more online shopping and I realised, 'Oh I actually like these [cuts] more. I like this type of outfit.'

S: I like straight-cut jeans, tight at the top and baggy at the bottom. And then a tight-fitted crop-top and then Air Forces.

Did you find that after lockdown, you wanted to change your look?

Both: Yeah, definitely.

L: That's what I did my English speech about, for my GCSEs. My speech was about actually finding your identity through clothes, which happened after lockdown for me. I talked about how different clothes can make you feel different ways.

Some people like to cover up by wearing a lot of baggy clothes, if they feel unhappy with their body or something else. But how it's good just to show yourself, and your identity, enjoy what you wear.

S: I always change my look. I go through phases. In 2019 I went through a skater phase. And then I was – do you know what VSCO [style] is?

The oversized tees and the water bottles and scrunchies.

S: Yeah. And now I don't know what my style is. It's more like . . .

L: —general.

S: Yeah, general. It's like, basic.

Do you think you'll ever settle on one look and think, 'OK, this is me now'? Or do you like the change?

S: I like the change.

Yeah, it makes it more fun. Is there an item of clothing or an outfit that's really popular at your school?

L: It depends. Our school is split up into the different genres of what people wear. Like you've got the trendy people. What are the other ones, Sofia?

S: Like, the girls who wear tracksuits and stuff. There's not one specific thing but in our age group, Juicy Couture tracksuits are really in right now. Velour, stuff like that.

Do you think teenagers in London dress differently from teenagers in other places?

S: I think London fashion is more about streetwear, and I think you can find that everywhere.

And what about here – do you think teenagers in Camden dress differently from teenagers you see when you go to other parts of the city?

Both: Definitely.

S: They're bolder and don't really care about what people think.

So when you say you change your style a lot, what do you think makes you want to change your style?

S: I think just what's in.

How do you know what's in, is it from people you know, or celebrities or . . . ?

S: I think social media. Like on TikTok, you see a lot of styles on there. When people go viral, it's mainly because of their style or look. It's really influential with teens.

So you see someone on TikTok and think, 'Well I could do or wear that too.'

L: Yeah, exactly. You just see a bunch of teenagers wearing different outfits and you think, 'Actually, that's quite pretty.' And then you try to find dupes of that clothing.

Do you ever see people on the street and think, 'Oh she looks amazing, I'd love to dress like her'?

L: Definitely. Sometimes that's what you want yourself – if I get dressed I'm like, that's what I want. Say you're walking through Oxford Street, you want someone to walk by and think, 'Oh I really want to dress like her!' It makes you feel really nice if someone comes up to you and says, 'Oh, where is your outfit from?' That makes you feel nice.

Do you ever ask people where their outfit is from?
L: Sometimes, but Sofia's the confident one!
[Both laugh]
S: Yeah, I usually ask people. And sometimes people come up to me and say, 'I really like your outfit,' and it makes me feel really nice, and I'm happy the whole day.

Do you think it's easier for girls or boys to dress well?
L: Girls.
S: Yeah, girls. They can count on each other. With guys, they copy their friends. And sometimes it's not in a good way. When they actually find out what they like to wear, then it changes and looks quite nice.

That's a question of confidence I think, and not everyone has that. It's all trial and error and finding what suits you.
S: For girls, you have a lot more options. Whereas I think guys are quite limited, they're stuck with t-shirts and jeans.

I think a lot of them probably would like more options, if there weren't so many rules. What do you think makes a boy well dressed?
S: I think every girl has their preference, but we both like the nineties style on guys: the baggy jeans and shirt that's quite baggy too.

L: Yeah, exactly. Baggy jeans. When their hair is – not long but like, curtains.

What do you wear to feel confident?

L: Flared jeans.

S: For me, it's really short crop-tops that are tight-fitted, with straight-cut jeans. That's what I'm most confident in.

Do you think that'll change as your style changes? Or will you keep that as something you can always go back to?

S: I think that it's a classic style, it'll never go out of trend. Whereas in the past, I used to wear stuff that was really in trend and I then had to give it all away or sell it when it was out of trend.

15. At Centre Point

The other day I heard the man in the hardware shop explain to one of my neighbours that the previous week's rain hadn't been like rain. It had been like a big machine in the sky, dumping rain on everything. Today it's so bad that the tourists opposite me on the bus are drenched through in their light summer separates, clutching only a cheap and flimsy Union Jack pocket umbrella. Immediately I recognise the umbrella as a purchase made under duress of downpour. A man two rows ahead is wearing a black plastic bag over his clothes. He's made a hole in the top for his head to stick out. It is astonishing to me, in a way, that neither the city nor its people think to make any preparations for the rain we know is inevitable. I watch the bus gliding through all these new puddles, making graceful arcs of water that soak the kerb. I am transfixed by them until the bus driver suddenly stops, turning the engine off. The route is terminating early because the road ahead is flooded.

Well, I'm already running late for therapy, so I scurry downstairs, repeating in my head a phrase that has brought me a lot of solace and motivation these past months: *OK, no problem. I will proceed on foot.* What this means is that I can go anywhere, do anything in this city, if I do it all under my own steam. It's an idea that has circled in my head since I moved here ten years ago – that I can make any kind of life I might want here, providing I do it myself. It's as true now getting off the 134 as it was a decade ago, arriving alone with my bags at Euston station.

Inevitably, my feet quickly meet groundwater and my New Balances are soaked through. Keep on going, I tell myself. I too am unprepared, like everyone else here, though at least I'm wearing a baseball cap. By the time I get to Tottenham Court Road I am submerged in it: the rain, yes, basically biblical in both quality and quantity, but also the way this city does not give a shit about it. Nobody here seems to own a decent umbrella. Nobody dresses appropriately. Every street I cross has a coursing river, a miniature Thames of its own, pulsing along its edges. The bottom of Centre Point forms a wind tunnel that blows my cap clean from my head – luckily, I know how to catch it, because it's not my first time at this particular rodeo. Ten years here, as I said. There was a report in the newspapers this week that said all of this is only going to get worse. The climate as we know it is breaking down, and all of us are going to have to live with the consequences. At least, I think the papers said this. I was too afraid to read them properly and I turned off the radio under the guise of self-care. Solace, motivation, whatever you want to call it: I think this city is going to need it in spades. Biblical quantities of it, wherever we might find it.

16. Walking

When the bus comes, I take a seat on the top deck. I do this so I can look more closely at the street, the flats over shops along Caledonian Road. I want to list everything I can see and hear, however incidental. From here I can see which buildings have mould, subsidence, cheap cream curtains. Which have been the subject of expensive makeovers, and what that means for the spirit of the street – to have these rich and not-so-rich neighbours living side by side. Most of London beyond my own neighbourhood is somewhat novel to me and as the bus routes travel mostly on main roads, they are a source of endless visual stimulation: restaurant signage, advertising hoardings, blue plaques, street signs pointing to unfamiliar districts, old leaves trapped in gutters, red brick walls turned dark grey from centuries of air pollution, an unexpected panel of stained glass, black soot on unloved façades.

In upper windows: office plants, halogen strip lighting, personal possessions, attractive vases, framed posters, a painted rainbow tacked to the glass, computer screens, replica Eames chairs, photocopiers, armchairs, the occasional cat, ironing boards, plastic carrier bags.

At ground level: dirt, mangy pigeons, an oven left out beside the council refuse bin, daisies and dandelions poking up between pavement slabs, a confetti of pink blossom petals lining the same in veins of pastel, D-locks waiting on bike racks.

And, without noticing, I identify the noise that washes over it: pneumatic drills, traffic hum, a fast-moving siren. Once I tune in to it, what is striking is how little of it comes from people on the street. The pedestrians' footsteps are almost silent, even when they move in hordes towards the traffic lights.

I don't know why I am doing this. Maybe it's an attempt to stave off the boredom of daily life here. It can be easy to accrue that daily boredom, and much more difficult to undo it. So I look for small, ordinary things, the things I would otherwise ignore, because life is made of these small things. If I can see them, list them in my mind, maybe I can make them stick.

No such luck. The things I see and hear from the top deck of the 17 will wash over me the same as anything else I might see or hear. Were it not for the list I am making in my notebook, I would forget them all the moment I step off the bus. Maybe the value is in the process itself instead, a form of undoing the accumulated dailiness, the complacency I've earned from seeing the same things, the same places. I am very caught up, usually, in the business of being alive. I forget how it all weaves together. Maybe I tend not to notice it in the first place.

I step off the bus near Holborn Circus. Now I am heading on foot through the centre of the City of London, on my way to an exhibition at the Barbican Centre. Here in the City there are traces of Roman London underneath so many layers of newness. There are scars from the Great Fire of 1666, and buildings constructed on World War II bombsites, and on top of that, the newest layer, the moneyed buildings which house the offices of banks and FTSE 100 companies.

There are no boundaries here, no walls or streets that separate the centuries from one another. Where I'm walking is close to the very centre of the capital. Not an inch of this land can afford to be wasted. The City is its own ceremonial county, with its own police constabulary and Lord Mayor. In terms of London's history, the City is packed more densely with historical fact and intrigue than anywhere else in the capital. Here, on one street corner, is the Golden Boy of Pye Corner: a small gold-plated statue of a round little child with his arms crossed, set into the side of a building on Cock Lane and Giltspur Street. The Golden Boy was put there in the late seventeenth century to mark the spot where the Great

Fire of London was stopped. Whoever made the statue made sure to render the child plump – 'prodigiously fat', as the memorial states, representing the 'sin of gluttony' that was the very cause of the fire. I pass through Smithfield Market, where a market for livestock and meat has operated for more than a thousand years. Now meat trading begins at 2 a.m. and finishes at 8 a.m., before I am even up and dressed. I like walking through these parts of London as they are a physical reminder of how much there is here outside of what I see and think about every day.

I round St Bartholomew's Hospital to reach Postman's Park. Postman's Park is a small green space in the grounds of a church, St Botolph's Aldersgate, overlooked on all sides by tall, more modern buildings. It's a place for passing through, and sometimes for stopping on a bench for a moment's rest or some quiet contemplation. The traffic roar from the nearby streets remains, but the park has a calm air, and feels a little like being inside a ceramic bowl. The central feature of the park is the Watts Memorial to Heroic Self-Sacrifice, a Victorian-era monument housed in a long, covered open veranda. Under the tiled canopy is a wall, lined with tablets, each commemorating an ordinary Londoner who lost his or her life attempting to rescue another. There among the tiles are Frederick Alfred Croft, who died under a train in 1878 trying to save a 'lunatic woman' at Woolwich Arsenal station, and William Donald, a nineteen-year-old railway clerk who drowned in the River Lea going after a boy caught in weeds there. Mary Rogers, stewardess of a boat named the *Stella*, gave up her lifebelt and went down with the ship in 1899, and Thomas Simpson saved many lives from thin ice on Highgate Ponds only to die of exhaustion in January 1885.

Named for its instigator, the Victorian artist George Frederic Watts, the Memorial to Heroic Self-Sacrifice is the kind of quaint curiosity you sometimes stumble upon when moving around a city like London. But its installation did not come about easily. Watts was an establishment artist and an idealist, with a deep-seated belief that art could be a force for good. In addition to his work painting and sculpting, he collected newspaper cuttings with stories of ordinary people who committed these exceptional acts of courage. With his wife Mary, he lobbied for the creation of a memorial like this – honouring everyday heroism – and in 1887 Watts wrote a letter to *The Times* suggesting it be built to commemorate the Golden Jubilee of Queen Victoria. Twelve years elapsed before Watts met the vicar of St Botolph's, and the pair launched an appeal to raise £3,000 to pay for the memorial. Fifty-three ceramic tablets, commemorating fifty-three acts of self-sacrifice, were installed. There is space remaining for many more, but only one has been added since, the first since the 1930s, for a man named Leigh Pitt who, in 2007, drowned saving a child in the canal at Thamesmead.

Making a life for yourself in a city where you didn't grow up involves a level of insulation you're not granted when you stay in your hometown. If you are young and lucky, and many who leave their hometowns for bigger cities are, living somewhere else can mean that years pass during which you rarely have to think about death. If all your friends and colleagues are similarly young and lucky, death can seem like something that happens elsewhere and to other people. I have thankfully only been to one funeral in London in the ten years I've lived here. I know that this won't be true forever. But it can be easy in a place like this to insulate yourself with a busy work life and ambition and a bustling social calendar. In an uncomfortable place, it can be easy to be consumed with notions of comfort over all else: financial comfort, physical comfort, the endless comfort of love and friendship. I am often consumed with my desire for comfort. How can I stop to think about the end of everything, when everything is so much in progress?

When the pandemic arrived in Britain, it brought with it fears of mass death and the visuals that accompany it – body bags in the streets, ambulances queuing all down the road. One worst-case scenario plan I heard on the radio involved contingency plans for a morgue in the open spaces of Hyde Park. I remember waking one morning and turning to look at Karl dozing beside me, listening to the news on the radio, wondering about the odds of one of us dying of the virus by the year's end.

Looking at the Memorial to Heroic Self-Sacrifice, I think of those who haven't survived the pandemic. The medics and delivery people and bus drivers and shop workers who knew they were putting their lives at risk in the course of their daily work but who kept getting up in the morning and going, and who lost their lives as a result. It doesn't take much these days to bring into sharp relief the madness of how much time and energy I seem to spend thinking about the surfaces of things, when these are the grey and serious depths that lie beneath.

I am thinking of how if I am safe now, it's in part because of what those people did. I did nothing. I stayed at home and ate the old cans of beans at the back of my cupboard, I social-ised on Zoom, I made only bi-weekly trips to the shop in the linen face mask I purchased on Etsy and rubbed my hands assiduously with hand sanitiser, before, during, after. It was the bare minimum, really. Eventually I got sick anyway, and later on I recovered, though my ribs have ached every day since then. And now I am here in Postman's Park. It is easy to forget, now that the city is open again, what it lost while it was closed, and who has been lost with it. I am thinking of how a city might manage to mark this loss, this sacrifice, made by so many.

There are other people in Postman's Park on this Thursday lunchtime. The park takes its name from the fact that in the nineteenth century, it was popular with workers from the General Post Office around the corner on King Edward Street, who enjoyed sitting in its greenery on their breaks. Today there are some people who look like they are trying hard to pass the time, wrapped up in many layers, listening with headphones on, drinking tea or coffee from takeaway cups. Under the veranda, a woman has left a handwritten letter and flowers for her late husband. I don't read the letter past the first line, because it feels too intimate, even though she has left it in this public space for a reason. I have the same motivation for not looking too closely at the other people in the park as I take my seat on a bench across from the memorial. Each is entitled to their privacy, I think, even as we choose to be here in public. I wrap my coat around me, because it is still cold for this time of year. It is good to be outside again, but maybe not for too long.

17. In Mayfair

At the corner of Old Bond Street and Burlington Gardens, just behind the Royal Academy, is the building that houses the only carillon in London. At street level the building is occupied by a Salvatore Ferragamo store that looks like any other luxury retailer along this strip; on its roof there is a tower containing the carillon, which is a set of church bells operated by a keyboard. Carillons are most typically found in market squares in Belgium and the Netherlands, and their playing and preservation there is recognised by UNESCO as intangible cultural heritage. In this part of the world, however, there are only a handful. Perhaps the English prefer a less complicated kind of bell tower. A plaque on the wall beside the glossy shop windows of Salvatore Ferragamo states that the carillon, known as the Atkinsons carillon, is played by hand on special occasions of public and private rejoicing.

The first time I read this plaque, I am curious about a number of things: who plays the bell, how can I get inside, why might London only have one carillon to begin with? What are the advantages of a carillon over another kind of bell tower? Most of all, I am wondering what occasions of public and private rejoicing might merit the ringing of the carillon's twenty-three bells.

Mayfair is a small corner of London, a little over one square kilometre. It has been an enclave for the city's wealthy residents since the 1600s and today it's generally used as a playground for the international super-rich, the people with the means and desire to shop for fine art and designer goods along one of the most expensive shopping streets in the world. For a little while I am here often, having taken a short-term job in the offices of a family jewellery company, writing a history of the brand. I take the bus in the morning and disembark on Regent Street; I sit at a desk all morning reading and typing. At lunchtime I reheat my leftover stew in the microwave before venturing out to the Mayfair streets for a short walk.

The plaque makes it seem quaint. Public and private rejoicing, I think, like the end of a war or maybe a monarch's birthday, if you were interested in celebrating that. The concept of public rejoicing itself felt like a relic from a different time: like the scars of the Blitz that are still visible in some parts of the city.

Soon after I first see the plaque, and the tower itself, the first lockdown is announced. After that, there is nothing to rejoice about, and at home, when I think of the carillon tower on Old Bond Street, I feel inexplicably lonesome. I picture the street empty and silent. The bells, I assume, will remain unplayed for a long time.

* * *

On the radio in the morning, the DJ likens the sudden onset of warm weather to the fall of a regime, and he is right. One year has passed. Outside, every bench in every park is full by noon, and some people have come equipped with camping chairs, yoga mats and picnic rugs. The first day of spring sunshine has coincided with a loosening of restrictions on outdoor gatherings, allowing parents to meet children and grandchildren again, footballers to kick balls around together, etc. It is only March, and already the desire lines etched by footfall into the grass look more like something seen at the tail end of the summer. Jubilation, of a kind, is here. It's a quiet jubilation, a slow sort of throat clearing, from a city that has been marked by grief and hurt over the last twelve months. Even when we acknowledged that it was temporary, the loss London suffered felt almost like an existential threat – shuttered restaurants, theatres under mothballs, offices with no workers, empty streets, empty streets, empty streets.

I look out the kitchen window. I will proceed on foot, I repeat to myself, lacing up my muddy runners once more and beginning the long walk into town. Out on the streets on my journey I see tie-dye dungarees, fashionable influencers with designer accessories, young men in shirts open perilously low swaggering to the park with bags of supermarket beer. Jeans more rip than fabric. Hijabs in spring pastels. Neon flashes on athletic gear, leggings and crop-tops and so on. Long prairie dresses with sleeves half-pushed up, like a window in a stuffy room that opens just the barest inch. On sunbathers I see bikini tops with unnecessary but enticing zips. Men who have exercised their right to forgo a shirt entirely. Flip-flops on feet that look in need of medical intervention. Maxi dresses in polka dot and floral prints, which look so new they should still have the fast-fashion price tags on. Also I see plenty of confused people, people like me who are slow to trust the good news. People who still wear thick scarves around their necks, or quilted gilets unzipped to let the warm spring air in.

Look good for the Great Return! admonishes a sign in a shop window on Great Portland Street. It's not something I've been thinking about much lately, looking good. I keep walking. When I reach the centre of the city, I find that it is still mostly asleep.

* * *

It is natural, I think, to want to use stories to make sense of the world. I felt this strongly during the first lockdown: the urge to take control of uncontrollable events by thinking of them in terms of the story we might someday tell about them: the beginning, the middle, the end. The beginning was clear. I'd just lived through it, and it was the only thing anyone was talking about. The middle was a mystery. But the end, I hoped, might be OK. It might even be a cause for celebration. I thought a lot about the Atkinsons carillon, standing alone and still above what I imagined as deserted Mayfair streets. No sports cars, no shopping bags. No uniform-clad doormen standing guard outside shopfronts, no tourists. I imagined the gates of the Burlington Arcade shuttered and padlocked. At a time when life, and the city, seemed so quiet, I thought about what it would be like to break the silence. The pealing of the bells high above the street. I thought it could mark some moment of ending, the turning of a page after the pandemic ended. I knew on some level that the pandemic would not end so cleanly, with all of us out in the street kissing each other and waving hankies like VE Day at the end of the war.

The quiet days also reminded me of being a teenager. The aimlessness of time at that age. When I was young I loved reading and rereading novels about cities, feeling with poignancy the distance between my own life and the splendour of 1980s Manhattan in books by Jay McInerney or Tom Wolfe. Mary McCarthy's *The Group* weaved city life and friendship together in a way that felt intoxicating. Those books had evoked a sense of place that felt so thorough that I'd wanted it for myself. I spent my teenage years waiting impatiently to find a city of my own, and a life in it. Something worthy of a good story.

I suppose some people might look at the movies, TV shows, books, and compare them relentlessly to their own lives. In that way, it must be hard for a single real life to measure up to the fiction. But I've never quite had that problem. Real life didn't have to be glamorous. Anything, I thought, could be romantic, as long as I had a notebook or my phone, somewhere to jot down whatever I'd thought of or seen that day. My own life could be as constructed and fascinating as anything I might see on television, if I were the one constructing it for myself. This was not about being a raconteur, turning myself into a series of tall tales for the purpose of the party. The story would be my own. All I wanted was a way to situate myself inside it.

My first job as a writer was party reporting: being sent to fashion and arts events in New York and told to talk to everyone, take notes, record quotes, annoy celebrities and various VIPs as much as possible. I was young and ambitious; I had absolutely zero shame or embarrassment. I didn't know these people. I had a flight home booked for six weeks' time. What, exactly, did I have to lose? Disappointment on my editor's face the following morning was a much more painful prospect than looking slightly stupid in front of a Victoria's

Secret model. It was an ingenious way to explore New York: finding rips in the seams and worrying my way into the heart of the glamour, clutching my Dictaphone and my notebook in my hand like a passport. I got to see ridiculous things: high fashion and dive bars, rampant self-importance at every turn. Ludicrous people to whom I could never relate but was nonetheless intrigued by. I was twenty-two, in fairness. I was intrigued by almost everyone in the world.

I kept doing this kind of work intermittently for the next few years or so, until shame and embarrassment did catch up with me. That part was inevitable. I was at a fashion week party in a Mayfair restaurant and I was exhausted, tired of the day itself and of the career I had found myself in. I was looking for a quote from one particular magazine editor, which would give me enough to write my article. Then I could leave and go and meet my friends in the pub. I was hovering around, being slightly annoying, obviously, because that was my job.

'Who is she?' I overheard the magazine editor asking her assistant, a stylist of some renown.

'God,' the stylist replied, rolling her eyes. 'I have no idea!' The two of them laughed, like mean teenage girls, knowing well that I could hear them, and I thought: this is ridiculous. This is not what I'm interested in at all. I picked up my notebook and left without waiting for the quote.

Outside, Mayfair was quiet. It was a Monday night in September and other than a few prowling SUVs waiting for passengers to leave nearby restaurants and hotels, I was alone. I walked down the street and felt light. I will proceed on foot: make a path, or find one that takes me through the city, the way I wish to go. That was private rejoicing, the relief of walking down Brook Street in the cold September night. The feeling of knowing myself on some deeper level, in a new way. The turning of a page. If I'd had a bell to hand, I would've been ringing it with delight.

* * *

The reality of it is that the reopening, when it does come, is neither great nor conclusive. Now the weather is warmer and I am walking again, heading once more for Mayfair. The times in my life when I came here with purpose and a destination in mind – an office, or an appointment – are alien to me now. Now I only ever seem to walk in this loose, directionless way. It's pleasant, but in the same way that being sent home from school is pleasant. It is a freedom that doesn't quite feel warranted, or right.

When I started to write this book, it had been some months since I'd walked the city freely in the way in which I was accustomed. The practice of Going Time – my easy and necessary rambling between one appointment and another, the connective thread that links together all my social and professional obligations – had been traded cleanly for short walks to the local supermarket, and longer ones around the tree-lined residential streets of my neighbourhood. I had always believed that with time I would return in some form to the normal city. But I have yet to do so. The months have advanced without my noticing, the end of my time writing this book is near, and I have conceded that this might have to be the normality I was waiting for. London reopened and to my knowledge there were no peals of jubilation from the Atkinsons carillon tower.

I am making up for lost time, I repeat to myself on the way into town, in a manner that makes me think of gritted teeth. The bus deposits me on Great Portland Street, and from there I cross town via a favourite route: Mortimer Street to Cavendish Square, then down the gentle valley of Wigmore Street, a road that always seems to catch sunlight on its slope. I know I will be walking for some time, and so my first destination is Paul Rothe & Son, the Marylebone sandwich shop with the pretty jam-laden windows. Inside, father and son make the sandwiches together, reciting orders from memory as customers order and pay up. The place is crowded with diners sitting on little folding seats, sharing a lunch hour. The sandwich men are kind and good-humoured in a way that means I would come back even if the sandwich were bad. But I know from previous experience that the sandwiches here are reliable – my ham and cheddar on granary bread, a little chilli relish, goes wrapped in paper into my bag, and I keep walking. On we go.

I round Manchester Square, another of the city's empty private garden squares, its gates locked and smelling of wee, then I head south to cross Oxford Street. Here on the main thoroughfare there is the enticing stink of Belgian waffles and roasted nuts. I dodge the visitors and shoppers and turn down a quiet side street into Mayfair. With fresh eyes I can see that all the modern iterations of money, the contemporary art galleries and designer names, have done nothing good for the atmosphere of this quadrant. Maybe I'm expecting too much from this neighbourhood, but I'm only interested in dusty corner shops under ancient awnings marked 'food and wine', the windows of antiquarian book dealers and independent jewellery traders, blue plaques marking the homes of generals and diplomats I have never heard of, little Italian delis with paintings of the Gulf of Naples on the walls and queues forming neatly outside.

This time I take routes I'm not familiar with, down lanes whose names I am surprised to read: Hay Hill, Haunch of Venison Yard. I try to let myself get lost, but inevitably end up back on Bond Street, staring up at the turreted tower of the Atkinsons carillon. I coast behind a well-dressed man in a beige linen coat, lingering in the wake of his expensive cologne for almost two blocks. I pace through the Burlington Arcade, past the windows of all the antique jewellers I used to examine on my lunch breaks in my last pre-pandemic office job. At Piccadilly it hits me: the glorious wealth of this place, the fact it is open to me and everyone else, the wide and flat road that will spirit you into the very heart of the city, the pulsing centre with its flashing billboards, its misidentified statue of Eros. The traffic always eddying past. A merry-go-round that does not stop. An infinite loop, a world without end.

I am keen to calm myself down now. It is hot in the sun; I have walked for too long. I am being ridiculous. I sit on the steps outside the Royal Academy to eat my sandwich. It is exactly what I need. Then I turn back to head north, via a route I know well. I trace a path up Savile Row. The street is lined with surnames that seem to embody Englishness. The men here, going in and out of the row's tailors or sitting outside a café with a little cup of espresso, all look fantastic. I think to myself that men have it easy, since they can look so put together with such little effort, until I see a young man open a copy of the *Financial Times* and shake it out with a flourish. He has his legs out in front of him, crossed nonchalantly at the ankle, and he's wearing a beautiful blue linen suit. The effortlessness is a ruse, I realise, and this man has spent more time on his appearance than I could even imagine.

Eventually I find a quiet pub on Margaret Street and take a seat inside. In a previous life, it's a place I'd come to for after-work drinks on a Friday, after a week of freelancing in a Soho agency. I would try to inveigle my way into steady employment through the rounds system and end up out of pocket and drunk on the 88 home. Today it is almost empty, the terracotta and blue floor tiles reminding me of ducking into the cool shade of a church on a foreign holiday. To write about the pub, or any pub, can feel like an imposition, like I'm taking something from the pub without permission. But this place will remain the same no matter what I write about it. Two men who don't know each other have started to chat at adjoining tables. They talk about their time living on and off the streets; one has the distant Irish accent that I have often heard on men of his age who left home a long time ago, and who have lived some hard years along the way. Closer to me, a pair of young people meeting for the first time on what seems to be a date, though they have mutual friends. The woman is hungover and seems nervous, knocking her glass of rosé across the table. Her date stands up, shaking the liquid from him. Clingfilm across his freshly tattooed leg saves it from damage. They move to a table outside to break the tension.

I came to this pub not to gawp at the other afternoon drinkers, but to gather myself after a long day on my feet. Also, to use the loo with the ease of the paying customer. From my handbag I take out my small notebook and pen. The other reason I came here was to write down the thoughts that had coagulated in my mind while I'd been walking. In writing them down, something begins to take shape. I write myself into the city in a way that felt only whispered while I was walking it. By definition, walking anywhere is close to passing through it, and the kind of walking I've been doing – no destination, no purpose, just looking – even more so. But the walking is just one half of it.

The other comes when I can sit, reflect, tell it back to myself. If I am waiting for the pealing of bells, the firing of the confetti cannons, I may be here for a long time. Rejoicing, whether public or private, can come gradually, in this small way: the opening of a door. Stepping, tentatively, outside.

Marlena Valles
Barrister

Last week you were fitted for your wig. Will that now be your only wig for your whole career?

Yes, until I'm a QC [most senior barrister] or a judge. And then you get a wig that's almost exclusively used for ceremonial purposes. Really long and curly.

I looked at the website for Ede & Ravenscroft, the legal dress supplier, and they have different wigs on sale. Some are more expensive.

Were you looking at the frizz-top?

Maybe?

Yeah, the frizz-top wig, I think it's sort of a historical anomaly. I've never seen one in person. There's the peak-front, too – I think it makes you look like Dracula.

There are lots of interesting barrister traditions surrounding the wig. Like wig bags. My pupil master, who was not a

QC, carried his wig to court in a red silk bag, embroidered with his initials. And I was like, 'Should I buy one of those?' He looked at me and said, 'You don't buy these for yourself.'

There are two colours of silk wig bags – blue and red. Only QCs are allowed to buy red ones. You can't just buy anything you want – I couldn't buy a QC's wig. Apparently the tradition is – I felt very embarrassed to not know this – when you do an excellent piece of work for a QC, the QC buys you a red bag. It's a big deal, because the QC might buy only one in their career, for the junior who impressed them the most. They present it to you, and they've had your initials put on it. And that's what you carry your wig to court in. Blue, I could buy now, but it's a bit naff to buy a blue bag because other barristers might look at me in the robing room and think, 'So she hasn't done a very good piece of work for a QC yet, I see.'

Is it correct that you will only wear your wig in court?
Yes, and this is very important. My chambers is about a five-minute walk away from the Royal Courts of Justice. So when I go over, I'll be wearing my normal suit with a white shirt. The shirt will be the kind you can wear collars and bands with, which is part of the barrister's uniform. The orthodox view is that you should not put on your band and collars or wear your gown while you're walking to court, and the same with the wig of course.

So you're walking across the road. You are not immediately recognisable as a barrister.

Yes. Some people take a more lenient approach to the rules and do wear court attire outside of court. You'll see it at the Pret across the road from the courts. That Pret is a hotbed of misbehaviour. But I think it all comes down to professional ethics and ensuring that barristers do not abuse their positions as officers of the law, in the same way that I can't use my professional email to make online purchases. The reason that you wear certain garments in court is because you are acting in this very particular capacity, and you'll diminish the importance of the uniform if you wear it to have a sandwich in Pret.

By contrast, even if QCs are scrupulously following the rules, you can usually discern from what they're wearing on the way to court that they're probably barristers.

What do they wear?

They wear this sleeved black waistcoat under their silk gown. But often they will continue to wear the waistcoat when they are outside court and that's not seen to be improper in the same way. It means you can tell who the really good barristers are when you're at the Pret! You know who to save the last salmon sandwich for.

So: underneath your robe you're wearing a particular kind of shirt.

Men wear shirts with detachable wingtip collars. In place of a tie, they wear bands, which are two white oblong pieces of cloth tied to the neck. The vast majority of women barristers will wear these little things called collarettes which are a sort of a bib, a mini-poncho that you wear over a dress, and tuck into your jacket. They're quite funny. The collarette is lace and is intended to give the appearance of the top third of a shirt.

I don't wear dresses, and so the 'ladies collarette' poses a problem. I am also six foot one and so I am too tall for any of the women's shirts available. Plus, they're really shit quality. Not to rant about the difficulty of obtaining professional workwear as a woman, but men can get a good-quality, work-appropriate suit and court shirt literally anywhere down Chancery Lane at really competitive prices. Whereas I have to have everything that I wear tailor-made, because first, there aren't that many designers that make dark women's suits, period, and second, of the designers that do make appropriate suits, women's sizing doesn't offer changes of inseam. It's astronomically expensive.

It's expensive and it's also complicated to get things tailor-made.

I never want to make barriers to access sound greater than they are, and the truth is I don't have any female friends who have the same issue that I have because they all wear dress suits, but I think that for me, as a lesbian, the way I see my gender is closely linked to my sexuality. Like, very much a woman, but a lesbian woman. It makes total sense to me in that context, but I think it's odd to be confronted on quite a regular basis at work with the fact that that's not a usual choice to make. Even though I think it's so normal to wear a suit as a woman [outside of the bar], everybody does it now.

So when other people say to you, 'Well, you could just wear a dress suit' . . .
I think that people don't get it, that they think 'Just because you're a lesbian you don't have to [wear a suit].' It's very hard for me to explain that I'm not comfortable wearing dresses, but not because I don't like being a woman – I love being a woman. I just like suits, and think I look good in suits.

How does it feel when you wear the wig?
It's a little bit uncomfortable, but I don't mind the discomfort. I actually don't mind barristers having to wear silly outfits. Putting on the outfit gives you the sense that there's a function that you're performing. And also you're not yourself – you put on a costume and you hopefully rid yourself of any kind of human ego or personal input into the case. A good barrister is ultimately a fungible entity. You should be able to swap one good barrister for another good barrister.

And how did you feel at the fitting? Did that feel like a milestone for you?
I'm very resistant to ever thinking anything is a milestone. I never feel particularly overwhelmed by a graduation or something like that. But one thing that did strike me is that my parents bought my wig. I have lived in the UK for more than a decade, but I am American, and my family still lives there. I don't come from a family of lawyers or academics,

and because the legal system in America is different, I didn't expect they would feel any inherent pride over the idea of their daughter being a barrister. But I was complaining to my mother about how expensive it was and she said, 'We'll buy your wig for you.' I then sent her a photo of me in the wig and she sent me back this long, incredibly touching reply. I couldn't have possibly expected that it would affect her in the way that it did.

Did her reaction change how you felt about the actual item?
It did, yes. It's imbued now with a sense of parental pride that I never thought a garment made with horsehair could be imbued with.

FIELD NOTES
SPRING

In the small newsagent's in Kentish Town
The man behind the counter pulls his Berghaus fleece tight around him and rubs his hands together. He calls outside, where another man fiddles with his phone.

'Dave, what's the score? Who's winning?'

'India, at the moment. England doing appalling.'

'Ah,' the newsagent says. 'That settles it. Today, I am Indian.'

Swain's Lane
Three uniformed removals men grappling with a ten-foot-high potted palm, lifting it out of a van with care, using a twisted blanket around the base of the pot.

Highgate High Street
Liam Gallagher, waiting for a lift.

Camden Town

A teenager in shiny black Dr. Martens, a purple Kappa jacket – vintage – and hair dyed down the middle, separated into two different hemispheres – pink and yellow, rhubarb and custard. He is half my age, and yet I feel an eerie sense of continuity when I pass him on Camden High Street. There were teenagers who looked like this when I was a kid, and maybe there will always be teenagers who look like this.

Museum Street

A burly delivery man in Super Mario blue overalls, pushing a dolly piled high with parcels down the street with great vigour. Two notes – a ten, a five – flutter from his pocket and land briefly on the wet pavement before another passer-by swoops on them and goes running after him in chase.

Leather Lane

A man in a gold Burberry puffer jacket and similarly coloured chinos pulls up on a slightly battered white Vespa with a sticker of a very sexy woman on the front. He walks up to the hatch of the coffee shop and asks, can he have a free coffee in exchange for putting a coffee shop sticker on his Vespa? And if not, could he pay for the coffee and just have a sticker anyway?

Waterlow Park

Man in his seventies wearing a flat cap and stylish Italian walking shoes, brown with turquoise panels, reading Philip Roth on a bench in the sunshine.

Portland Place

An elderly lady emerging from one of those fantastic grand apartment buildings near Regent's Park, walking slowly in brown heels and fawn-coloured cashmere skirt and cardigan, hair dyed a rich burgundy brown, large pearl orbs in each ear.

Islington industrial estate

A shaven-headed builder in a black t-shirt and yellow hi-vis vest sitting on the pavement with legs outstretched, eating a box of fried chicken with palpable gusto.

A Highgate side street

A teenager with long unruly hair and wearing a brown school uniform pauses alongside a parked car, turns and looks over her shoulder – first right, and then left – carefully checking her reflection in the window.

Borough High Street

Woman in a lime-green shift dress with brassy gold buttons on the hip pockets causes a taxi to honk its horn in consternation while she poses for a photo in the middle of the street.

The Hayward Gallery, South Bank

Two young mothers push tiny babies in buggies. One woman is in double denim, the other in rust-coloured maternity cords. Both have shiny ponytails and fluorescent New Balance sneakers. The gallery is quiet, and they shake with silent laughter over a shared joke, gripping each other by the arms.

18. Walking

It is early on Sunday morning and there is nothing to eat in the flat, so I put on my jacket and head towards the supermarket for yoghurt and granola. The street is empty. Everyone is inside, asleep, and only their well-kept gardens of tulips and magnolias stand sentinel as I pass. It's the earliest cusp of summer, and I am alone in London again, out on the street but also inside a room built from the fierce privacy of my own thoughts.

This is a room of my own that I am always making and remaking. This is where I tend to disappear into when bored in a meeting, zoning out and finding myself once again in the familiar environs of my mind. The door I open when squeezed onto a packed Tube carriage, in an attempt to make a little inner space for myself. I come back to this room whenever the city is loud and the demands on my time and energy feel endless. This empty room of mine, which I furnish at will with my memories, desires, worries.

At the centre of this room there is a scale model of a city. At first glance, it will resemble the real city I inhabit: the same buildings, landmarks, all bisected by the river at its centre. But I can see that certain things are out of proportion – some buildings magnified and blown up, others entirely absent, like a bomb was dropped on them. The effect is uncanny in its familiarity, its differences. This model is the private city I have built for myself in the years I have lived in London. It is put together using memory and meaning. It exists for me alone.

I think that everyone who lives in a place like this will do this in some way – assemble for themselves a version of it that makes sense for them and them alone. We don't construct our private cities for fun or for pleasure. I make mine in order to survive living somewhere that is so large, so full, so teeming with the lives of others. I shore myself up with places and memories to give myself a feeling of belonging, a ballast against loneliness.

The flats I've lived in and offices I've worked in. The bus routes and Tube stations and cafés and corner shops. The homes of friends and the locations of parties. The summer spent working in a converted warehouse on Redchurch Street, and the fierce contrast I felt between the pittance I was earning and the expensive shops that lined the street below the office window. The daily packed lunch I ate on the steps at Arnold Circus, under a canopy of leaves. The curved glass panels of the pub in Holborn where I met my friends on my first weekend in the city, a brisk November night, a cheap pint of lager before we folded ourselves back into our coats and walked to catch the British Museum's late opening hours. The light streaming through those glass panels when I next came, with Julie, on an autumn afternoon two years later. The man in the kebab shop who refuses to let any of his colleagues make my order, only him. The bookshop I had a panic attack in. The rooftop I watched a sunset from, just two weeks ago. The back gardens of friends where we get silly with drink in the sun, making plans for the next weekend and the weekend after, which will never come to fruition. The flat where my aunt and uncle live, where I know I can always go if I need to. The offices, all over the city, that soaked up my time and gave me a living in return, and some-times threw in some good friends along with it. The view from the roof terrace of one of those offices – ridiculous, fourteen storeys up, the city split along its river seam and the Shard and St Paul's just a stone's throw from my perch. I felt like I should have been paying money to sit there, which is a belief only the privatised city can beat into you. The address of a friend's flat where I'd spent hours, possibly days, on her sofa and at her kitchen table, before our friendship ended abruptly when she left the country. Even though we weren't close anymore, I was not going to forget her post-code any time soon.

The favourite pubs, their beer gardens and booths becoming as familiar over the years as my own living room. The preferred cubicle in the changing rooms of Parliament Hill Lido – painted a cheering yellow, a little celebration for myself before I take to the water. The guy at the corner shop who takes such joy in discussing the weather with me each time I go in that I learn to take joy in it too – first just to be polite and humour him, and then more genuinely, to canvass him for his opinion on what tomorrow might bring for us. The falafel shop in Clerkenwell I point out to Karl each time we pass it, reminding him of the time it gave me food poisoning on his birthday. The sandwiches eaten on park benches, their paper wrapping unfurled on my lap. The newsagent in Bloomsbury with its proud pictures of the time Rihanna stopped by, printed off from their CCTV cameras and sellotaped up by the till. The statue of Eros at Piccadilly Circus, where in a hurry I signed my name as witness to a friend's mortgage application, working my way into her life in an indelible fashion that made us both smile. The street corner where I met Stevie for the first time, and when I left, found myself thinking: I hope I can be friends with her for a very long time.

All the streets where I found myself struck dumb by something – where I suddenly saw or thought of something that would serve to change my mind and perhaps my life. How the light bending through the trees at Cavendish Square could cause me to rethink decisions, focus my energies on something new, decide to spend my time differently. The lavish hotel room where I interviewed a renowned artist, very clearly under the influence of sedatives, who praised me for my 'extremely calm energy', and how for a few months I let this praise trick me into thinking that I did indeed have extremely calm energy. The roti I ate on cold winter nights, in restaurants where my breath and the steam from the cooking fogged up the windows. The routes I run looping through quiet streets lined with multi-million-pound mansions, never seeing a soul except for private security in parked cars. A night out I foolishly left alone, drunk, and wandered alone through a network of empty Fitzrovia side streets at the witching hour until I found the bus stop. The Greek restaurant in Camberwell where I tried to ignore my stomach ache and enjoy my dinner. The night buses that always took me home safely, wherever I was in the city. Just a few more stops now.

I have built my private city without realising it, with every footstep on the pavement, every glance around me, every chance encounter. It has all added up without my noticing. I look at the city and I learn how it works, and in turn, it sees me, learns about me. London takes parts of me and holds them inside. 'The truest city is the most private,' writes Jonathan Raban in *Soft City*. My scale model is imaginary but it is also more real for me than any physical street corner. A building I once lived in could fall tomorrow. The palace of memory I've built within will always exist in the privacy of my thoughts.

How did I ever think it could be any different? When I came here I had no idea the emotional toll that comes with constructing a life for oneself. Every single street corner, every blessed night spent with friends, every encounter came with a price of its own. How could I take so much from the city – the friendships, the pleasure, the profit, the memories – and expect not to give anything of myself in return? What I find now, after ten years, is that the city is liable to remind you at unexpected moments of your past failures as much as your victories. Inopportune moments, too: I am walking down Old Compton Street with a new colleague when my toe catches lightly on the kerb and I stumble. I catch myself before I trip, and laugh lightly when Sarah asks me if I'm alright. I am, but I'm reminded of a night years earlier, when I did fall on a street like this and gashed my knee, hurt my pride badly though I tried to laugh it off then. Now there is a rush of feeling that comes back to me like the onset of an illness, and it takes until we get to the Tube station at Tottenham Court Road for me to feel myself again.

'We see ourselves in this city every day when we walk down the sidewalk and catch our reflections in store windows, seek ourselves in this city each time we reminisce about what was there five, ten, forty years ago, because all our old places are proof that we were here,' Colson Whitehead writes in *The Colossus of New York*. 'One day the city we built will be gone, and when it goes, we go. When the buildings fall, we topple, too.' Whitehead was writing a form of communal elegy about

Manhattan, where he grew up, in the wake of September 11, 2001. And I know that some elements of my private city can't last, either. It doesn't need to take a catastrophe. There are pubs that close without fanfare, reopening months later as even more metro supermarkets. The locations of former jobs or flings are repurposed, sometimes even demolished entirely to be reborn. But the private city can feel so real to me, so concrete, that I can't imagine it disappearing the same way.

The only way I can see it falling apart is if I leave. I would put both time and space between myself and my memories of London, and then I'd risk letting the private city in my mind crumble. I used to think that I would need to leave this place before I could complete it, that I'd end up moving away from London before I could wring every drop from it. One day my time would be up, regardless of whether I felt ready to say goodbye or not. But people leave every day having had enough. When they go, they take the private city with them, in the knowledge that it might start to disintegrate in their hands the moment the train pulls away from the station.

And so I keep mine alive by visiting it. I tend to it with every familiar walk around the neighbourhood, every Tube journey, leaning against the pole as the carriage rocks. Visiting the private city in this way has the same looping constancy of a dream, the same feeling of watching a baggage carousel turn and turn as the luggage on the belt appears and disappears. Some things are taken away, some stubbornly remain for cycle after cycle. My own life might change, but the city welcomes the most immutable parts of myself, the parts that are always the same. Here there is space for them. For this reason, the private city must remain private. I know the disappointment of trying to share it with an old friend or a new flame, bringing them to a favourite spot and waiting for them to share in my own personal pleasure of place. I see the way their eyes fail to light up.

'It's lovely,' says one of my oldest friends, when she visits for the weekend. 'I can see why you like it here.'

And I wish she meant it, but I know it's not the same for her, or for anyone but me. There is a certain loneliness in that, the sense that we spend so much time cultivating a complex reflection of ourselves – and then cannot show it to anyone else. This is a second-order loneliness. It is different from the one I try to protect myself from with the intricate webs I might spin. This is the inevitable loneliness of being alive, the same one I can sense walking alone in the early morning through the empty neighbourhood. Nothing happens to me on my way to the supermarket. I see nothing of interest, encounter nobody who might give colour to my writing or a shape to my thoughts. Even the supermarket itself is eerily quiet, just the self-service checkouts beeping quietly, speaking to themselves.

On the way home, tub of yoghurt in my tote bag. Still the street is empty. Nothing pressing to think about, really. Just my own problems, my memories, my desires and fears and preferences. This constant of mine, wherever I go. My light cotton jacket around my shoulders, my neon running shoes pulsing in and out of my field of vision below me. Perhaps this is what I have found here, this one version of myself that lies beneath it all. A permanent, unflinching thing. It's beautiful, this space of mine, and it belongs to me.

A note on the font

Hoefler Text, an old-style serif font that takes its cues from a range of classic fonts such as Garamond and Janson, was designed by Jonathan Hoefler and released in 1991 by Apple Computer Inc. (now Apple Inc.).

Released free with every Mac during the growth of desktop publishing, at a time when producing printed documents was becoming dramatically easier, Hoefler Text raised awareness of type features previously the concern only of professional printers. *New York* magazine commented in 2014 that it 'helped launch a thousand font obsessives'.

Acknowledgements

First of all I am indebted to Sophie Missing for her steadfast belief in this book from the outset, and to Marigold Atkey for her care and attention in shepherding it into being. Thanks also to all at Daunt for their help in taking this book from Word document to physical object. I am immensely grateful to Seren Adams for her careful eye and her constant support in my writing.

Before there was a book, there was an email newsletter, and thank you to the readers of the London Review of Looks for coming with me, metaphorically, on many of these walks. In particular, Dr Rosie Findlay has been an attentive and generous reader of my newsletters, and her academic analysis of the London Review of Looks contributed to my thinking while writing this book.

For logistical support, thank you to Claire Jermany of TFL and the Holly Lodge Community Group. Thanks also to James Vincent, and Bridget and John.

ACKNOWLEDGEMENTS

A huge thank you to my parents, Eilis Boland and Patrick Kinsella, for everything, ever, and in particular for giving me their own love of cities big and small and the lives we make for ourselves within them. My own friends and neighbours have been essential to my ability to make a good life for myself in London over the years – thank you all so much. Lastly, thank you to Karl McDonald for never turning down a walk and a chance to see what the world has to show us.